Amazing Stories to Tell and Retell ▪ 3

Amazing Stories to Tell and Retell ▪ 3

Lynda Berish
Marie-Victorin College

Sandra Thibaudeau
Marie-Victorin College

Houghton Mifflin Company
Boston ▪ New York

Director of ESL Programs: *Susan Maguire*
Senior Associate Editor: *Kathleen Sands Boehmer*
Developmental Editor: *John Chapman*
Editorial Assistant: *Kevin Evans*
Project Editor: *Anne Holm*
Senior Manufacturing Coordinator: *Priscilla J. Abreu*
Marketing Manager: *Patricia Fossi*

Cover design and image: Harold Burch Designs, NYC

Photo credits: p. 9, John Kenney/Montreal Gazette; p. 17, left: Todd Powell/The Picture Cube; right: AP Photo/Craig Field/Freefall Photography; p. 23, right: Network Productions/The Image Works; p. 33, UPI/Corbis-Bettmann; p. 40, John Kenney/Montreal Gazette; p. 51, AP/Wide World Photos; p. 56, AP Photo/Eric Draper; p. 57, left: AP Photo/Eric Draper; right: Chang W. Lee/NYT Pictures; p. 71, © Monkmeyer/Gottleib; p. 86, Luigi Facciuto; p. 87, Luigi Facciuto; p. 92, Caroline Hebard; p. 93, Caroline Hebard; p. 109, body: Photodisk; hand/mouth signatures: Naum Kazhdan/NYT Photos; p. 120, John Neubauer/PhotoEdit; p. 127, Jim Wilson/NYT Pictures; p. 153, left: James Pearson/NYT Pictures.

ACKNOWLEDGMENTS

"How a Power Drill Saved a Life." Used by permission of Luc Larouche, Dr. Roman Andrusiak, and Dr. David Miller. "He's Alive!" Used by permission of Joel Reignier and Luc Parent. "X-Sports." Used by permission of Murray Nussbaum. "Getting Pierced." Used by permission of Pierre Black. "Never Stop Moving." Reprinted by permission of Luigi Facciuto. "Search-and-Rescue Mom." Reprinted by permission of Caroline Hebard. "Can You Copyright Paradise?" Used by permission of Roberto Di Tommasso. "A Prescription for Mozart." Used by permission of Don Campbell. "Diving for Treasures." Used by permission of George Parry. "Do You Speak My Language?" Used by permission of Maria Dias.

Printed in the U.S.A.

Library of Congress Catalog Card Number: 98-71985

ISBN: 0-395-94913-0

6 7 8 9-FFG-08 07

Contents

www.hmco.com/college

Introduction

Amazing Stories to Tell and Retell 3 is an adult reader for students at the intermediate language levels. The book is designed to get students reading—and talking! The unusual topics of these human-interest stories capture students' attention and make them want to find out more.

Amazing Stories consists of ten units, each of which contains a pair of thematically linked stories. All units follow an identical format. A series of activities before each story is used to pique students' interest and to build background for the reading passage. Follow-up activities after each story help students better understand what they have read and also provide opportunities for vocabulary expansion. The unit wrap-up, called Put It Together, presents a language review and helps students make connections between the stories and the outside world. A key feature of the Put It Together section is the Tell the Stories activity, which guides students as they tell the stories in their own words, first to another student and then to someone outside the class.

THE STORIES

Every story in *Amazing Stories* is true. Over the years, we have collected these unusual anecdotes from magazines and newspapers and used them to motivate our students to read and to discuss what they had read. As we put the book together, we contacted and interviewed as many of the people in the stories as possible to check that the information was accurate and to discover other aspects of the tales that would add spice to these already remarkable stories. We would like to offer our heartfelt thanks to all the people who shared their stories. They were all extremely helpful, and their willingness to have their experiences included in this book will mean a lot to all the students who use it.

THE UNIT FORMAT

Each unit follows a set format.

- The unit opens with a Let's Get Ready page that stimulates students' interest and gets them involved in the unit. One aim of this section is to explore students' prior knowledge of the topic. New vocabulary is introduced, and students are often asked to make predictions about the readings that follow.

- Immediately preceding the opening of each story is a Before You Read section, which contains vocabulary work, categorizing activities, and discussion questions.

- The Reading Skills section that follows each story comprises many different types of activities. The most commonly used tasks involve general reading comprehension and vocabulary building and reviewing. However, several other types of exercises are featured. Among them are Scan for the Details, Vocabulary in Context, Focus on the Exact Information, Use the Context to Find the Meaning, Understand Fact and Opinion, Understand the Main Ideas and Details, Arguments for and Against, and Classify the Examples.

- The Put It Together section at the end of each unit contains several summary activities covering both stories. Let's Review provides a review of the events and vocabulary in the two stories. Tell the Stories helps students integrate the new language by telling the stories in their own words. They are given a variety of prompts and suggestions to make this process fun and interesting. Talk About It provides questions useful for group discussion.

- Two other features appear in the Put It Together sections. Beyond the Stories contains activities that help students make connections between the stories and their own communities. Writing Option suggests ideas for written follow-ups related to the unit topic.

TELL AND RETELL

One key feature of this book is the way it enables and encourages students to tell and retell the stories. This activity stems from the desire most of us have to share unusual or interesting stories we hear. Students are led through a series of steps that help provide the understanding of the story and the language practice they need to feel confident telling the story.

- First they read the stories and do the reading and language exercises that accompany them.

- Next they each tell the story to a peer in class. This provides an opportunity for sheltered practice.

- Then the student is invited to tell the story to an English speaker outside of class.

These retellings serve two purposes. First, as students talk about what they have read, they integrate the new language and make it their own. Second, the out-of-class retellings provide students who are embarrassed to speak English or who feel they have nothing interesting to say in English an opportunity to feel proud of their ability to tell an unusual or funny story. After practicing the story, students leave the classroom speaking English.

SOME TIPS ON TELLING AND RETELLING

The stories in this book can be used in many different ways. The activities outlined provide a basic framework. The teacher can then build on this framework to meet the needs of students of different ages, interests, and cultural backgrounds.

- Teachers may wish to survey the stories with the class and then allow students to select the one they think is best for them, or teachers may assign partners to work on a story together.

- When they are ready to tell the story to each other, students will be able to help each other remember details and vocabulary and formulate the sentences they need. Contrary to what we may think, students do not get bored telling the same story more than once. They appreciate the chance to practice their new language and build confidence in speaking English.

- Another classroom activity can involve having each student tell the story to another student who did not read it. During this phase, teachers should encourage the listener to be an *active* listener, asking questions and discussing the story afterward.

- Another option is to have students tell the story they heard, not the one they read. This encourages active listening and provides additional oral practice.

- Here are some other possibilities.
  1. Have students record the stories on tape and listen to themselves speak.
  2. Ask students to tell the story to the teacher first and then to another student.
  3. Suggest that students write out the story in their own words before they tell it.

- After the classwork is finished, the final step is for students to tell the story to someone outside the class. If students have difficulty finding an English speaker to converse with, teachers can help them find ways to structure this activity.
  1. Have students visit another classroom and tell the stories to students there.

2. Arrange lunchtime or after-school activities where English speakers will be present.
3. Have students visit a community center or senior center where they will have a chance to practice speaking English and telling the stories.

RATIONALE

The approach used in *Amazing Stories* is from the communicative model of language learning. It teaches reading strategies through a variety of interactive activities. Students work with partners to reinforce language and to help the other person learn. The dynamic classroom atmosphere that this creates draws students into focusing on content rather than on discrete aspects of language.

Reading skills are supported through a careful progression of activities. Pre-reading activities help students get started. Thematic units help students focus on content. The telling and retelling component gives students a real purpose for reading since they have a specific goal—to tell the story to someone else when they are through. This helps them to read with more interest and to remember more of what they read.

Amazing Stories builds vocabulary and reading skills through reading strategies, such as skimming to find the main idea and scanning for details. The methodology aims to develop students' confidence as readers and to build vocabulary in a supportive environment with the help of interesting, interactive exercises.

ACKNOWLEDGMENTS

We wish to thank:

- Kathy Sands Boehmer, who encouraged us through the writing stages and gave us valuable feedback about the stories
- Susan Maguire, who suggested these books and inspired us to write them
- Lauren Wilson, who found people and places for us and helped us with permissions
- John Chapman, whose enthusiasm and skillful editing helped shape the final product
- Allen Dykler, who gave us support and encouragement

We gratefully acknowledge our reviewers for their valuable input and suggestions. Thanks go to the following people:

Jesus Adame, El Paso Community College, Texas
Ann Bliss, University of Colorado, Boulder

Marcia Edward Cassidy, Miami Dade Community College, Florida
Linda Elkins, ESL, Houston
Rachel Gader, Georgetown University, Washington, D.C.

Special thanks also go to:

- Vicki Myrianthis for putting us in touch with Luigi, and for continuing to inspire her students to achieve their best.
- Our loving families, whose patience allowed us to spend many hours at our computers: Johnny, Tara, and Andrea Berish; Charles Gruss, Jean-Baptiste, Gaby, Annabel, Shem, and baby Tasnim
- Millicent Goldman for providing us with a constant supply of newspapers and magazines, where we found many of the stories, and Max Goldman for his keen proofreading

We also gratefully acknowledge the following people, for giving us permission to tell their stories:

- Dr. Roman Andrusiak

- Dr. David Miller

- Luc Larouche

- Joel Reignier

- Luc Parent

- Murray Nussbaum

- Andrea Berish

- Pierre Black

- Luigi Facciuto

- Caroline Hebard

- Linda Fabris

- Roberto Di Tommaso

- Don Campbell

- George and Catherine Parry

- Maria F. Dias

This book is dedicated to Doreen Jospe, for her courage.

Lynda Berish
Sandra Thibaudeau

Amazing Stories
to Tell and Retell ■ 3

Against the Odds

STORY 1   HOW A POWER DRILL SAVED A LIFE

STORY 2   HE'S ALIVE!

Let's Get Ready

A. You are going to read two stories about miraculous survivals—one in which human intervention saved a life and one in which fate and fast thinking saved a life. Both took place in remote areas. Discuss the following questions in groups.

1. What parts of the world are dangerous?

2. Why are these places dangerous?

3. How can people protect themselves in these places?

4. Do you think people generally are responsible for what happens to them?

5. Do you know anyone who was "born lucky"? Explain.

6. Did anything lucky ever happen to you? What happened?

B. Look at the list of places below. Discuss two dangers you would associate with each place.

- Central Park in New York City
- hiking trails in New Hampshire
- ski slopes in the Alps
- underground mines
- the Arctic
- tropical jungles
- construction sites

1

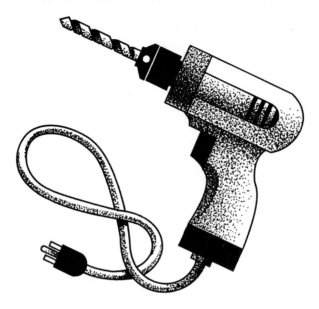

Before You Read

Complete the paragraphs using the words listed.

land
rooms
emergency
surgery
~~northern~~
remote
city
clinic
plane
people

The Arctic is around the North Pole. It is the most (1) ___northern___ part of the earth, and it is very (2) _____. The native (3) _____ are called Inuit. Puvirnituq is a small village in the Arctic. There are doctors in Puvirnituq, but they work at a small (4) _____ without operating (5) _____. When people need (6) _____, they fly to a big (7) _____ hospital in Montreal or Toronto. To reach the Arctic, people travel by (8) _____. But sometimes the weather is bad, and planes can't (9)_____. In a medical (10) _____, there can be problems.

How a Power Drill Saved a Life

The day Dr. Roman Andrusiak hurried into a repair shop to borrow a power drill, it wasn't to fix something in his house. Dr. Andrusiak was thinking of a patient's life. He thought he should have a power tool—just in case. As it turned out, the drill was what he used to save Luc Larouche's life.

The story began in the Arctic in a remote village with few medical facilities. It began when Luc Larouche was hit on the head by a rock. He was taken to the family doctor, Roman Andrusiak, for help. As Dr. Andrusiak examined the patient, he realized that Larouche needed an operation immediately to save his life. But there was no surgeon at their small clinic who could perform the specialized surgery.

Dr. Andrusiak consulted his colleague, Dr. David Miller, and they decided to call surgeons at the Montreal General Hospital for advice. The Montreal surgeons confirmed that the problem was urgent and said Larouche should be transferred to Montreal for immediate surgery. But the Arctic village was twelve hundred miles away, and it was completely fogged in. No plane could land that night.

Dr. Andrusiak knew that the situation was critical. If they couldn't stop the pressure building in Larouche's brain, the patient would stop breathing. Dr. Andrusiak turned to Dr. Miller, and they made a quick decision. They would have to operate. "We're family doctors—brain surgery isn't part of our experience," Dr. Miller explained later. "But this was a life and death situation. We knew we had to do something. Larouche had only a few minutes left."

The clinic didn't have a real operating room, so they put up curtains around the patient. They didn't have the specialized equipment available in larger city hospitals either. The doctors checked a medical textbook. Then, with the help of a small nursing team, they began to operate. Dr. Andrusiak took the power drill and carefully made a hole in the patient's skull to relieve the pressure. Blood rushed out and then kept pulsing and gushing. So large was the collection of blood that, to get it all out, a bigger hole had to be made in the skull. Dr. Andrusiak pulled off pieces of bone that the rock had broken and cleaned out the inside of the skull. After wrapping a bandage around the huge hole in Luc's head, he and two nurses put Luc onto a small plane and took off into the fog. By the time they landed, Luc was waking up.

Today Luc Larouche is playing piano and feeling as well as ever, thanks to the quick thinking of a handful of people in the Canadian far North.

Reading Skills

FOCUS ON THE EXACT INFORMATION

Answer the questions with exact information from the story. Use the number of words suggested.

1. What did Dr. Andrusiak use to save Luc Larouche's life? (3 words)

   He used _____ *a power drill* _____.

2. How was Luc Larouche injured? (3 words)

   He was hit on the head _____.

3. What did Larouche need immediately? (1 word/3 words)

   He needed an _____ to _____.

4. What did the surgeons at the Montreal General Hospital say? (2 words)

   They said that the problem _____.

5. What advice did Dr. Andrusiak and Dr. Miller get from the surgeons? (2 words)

   Larouche should be transferred to Montreal for

   _____.

6. Why were planes unable to fly that night? (2 words)

   The airport was completely _____.

7. What would happen if the doctors couldn't stop the pressure? (3 words)

   The patient _____.

8. What wasn't part of the family doctors' experience? (2 words)

_____

9. How did they create an operating room? (3 words)

They put up curtains _____.

10. How did they relieve the pressure in Larouche's brain? (4 words)

_____ in the patient's skull.

11. Where did Dr. Andrusiak put the bandage? (4 words)

_____ in Larouche's head.

12. What was happening by the time the plane landed? (2 words)

Luc Larouche was _____.

VOCABULARY IN CONTEXT

Underline the correct words to complete the paragraphs.

Puvirnituq is very far from any large cities. It is a (1. far, <u>remote</u>, distance) village in the Arctic. Sometimes the weather is bad, and the village is (2. fogged in, frozen in, fog). In this situation, planes can't (3. to arrive, arrives, arrive) or leave. When there is an (4. emergent, emerges, emergency), the situation can be (5. critical, crisis, critic).

When Luc Larouche was hit on the head by a rock, the doctors knew the patient had to be (6. transfer, transferred, transfers) to a large hospital. They knew Luc could stop breathing if (7. presses, pressure, to pressure) built up in his brain. It was a life and death (8. decide, decides, decision). If they didn't operate, Luc would stop (9. breath, to breath, breathing). Fortunately, the doctors were able to save Luc's life with the help of an (10. ordinary, ordinarily, ordinaries) power drill. They used the power drill to make a hole in Luc's (11. brain, skull, incision). Thanks to the doctors' quick thinking, the medical team saved (12. time, money, a life).

BUILD YOUR VOCABULARY

Are these pairs of words synonyms *(two words with the same meaning)* or antonyms *(two words with opposite meanings)?* *Write* S *for* synonym *or* A *for* antonym.

1. confirm	agree	S
2. rescue	save	S
3. operation	surgery	S
4. remote	close	A
5. urgent	critical	S
6. immediately	in a while	A
7. specialized	ordinary	A
8. medical facilities	hospital	S
9. location	place	S
10. fix	repair	S

Before You Read

A. What do you know about mountain climbing? Read these sentences with a partner and write **T** *for* **true** *or* **F** *for* **false.**

1. Experienced mountaineers can always avoid avalanches. _F_

2. Storms can occur without much warning in the mountains.

   _T_

3. Avalanches happen only in high mountains like the Rockies or

   the Alps. _T_

4. When an avalanche stops, the snow freezes solid very quickly.

   _T_

5. It is a good idea to sleep to conserve energy if you are lost in

   the snow. _F_

6. Most people who are buried in an avalanche will survive. _F_

B. Skim the text to check your answers.

He's Alive!

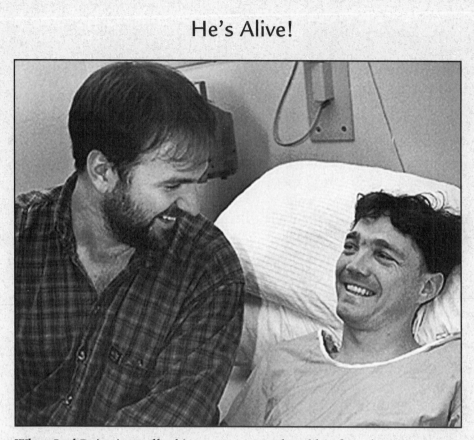

When Joel Reignier walked into a parking lot at the base of New Hampshire's White Mountains, the people gathered there couldn't believe their eyes. Hours earlier on the mountain Joel had been swallowed by an avalanche! No one expected to see him alive. But Joel survived the avalanche and lived to tell the tale. Rescue workers say it was a miracle, but Joel Reignier says, "I was just lucky."

Joel and his friend Luc Parent were both experienced hikers and mountain climbers. Joel grew up in the French Alps. He and Luc had hiked the White Mountains many times, and this hike began like any other. They had set out in good spirits, joking that the snack bars they had packed for energy were called Avalanche.

It began as a routine Sunday hike, but suddenly Joel and Luc realized that something had changed. "It was getting dark. The wind began to blow really hard, and we were sinking up to our waists in the snow," Joel says. Then, as Luc watched in horror, he saw his friend disappear down the mountain in a rush of snow. "I was pulling myself up with my ice ax, and I put my foot in the wrong place," remembers Joel. "All of a sudden I began to fall. I thought 'This can't be happening.' I was sure I was going to die." Luc remembers too. "I heard a scream and saw Joel falling down the mountain. He slid right by me. Then he disappeared." Luc shakes as he recalls the incident. "I called him, but he didn't answer. I didn't think he would survive."

Joel was carried by the snow 150 feet down the mountain. Although the fall took only seconds, it felt like hours. When he landed, Joel was buried up to his chin in snow. "I couldn't breathe. There was snow in my mouth, so I spit it out," he says. "I was stuck and I didn't know what to do. I only knew that snow could freeze in a few minutes. I tried not to panic." Suddenly, Joel realized that he had the answer. His right arm was free from the

snow and amazingly his ice ax was still attached to his wrist!

Joel worked frantically to chip away at the ice and snow. Finally he was free! He made a snow cave under a rock and crawled inside to wait for morning. Meanwhile, unaware that his friend was alive, Luc found shelter under a bush. Neither of them went to sleep. As experienced mountaineers, they knew that if they went to sleep, they might not wake up.

In the morning, both Joel and Luc began to struggle down the mountain. Neither of them knew if the other was alive. Luc followed a path and got to the bottom of the mountain at nine o'clock in the morning. Joel, with his ankle throbbing painfully, leaned on two sticks to help him move. Sliding, crawling, and rolling in the snow, he inched his way down the mountain. Seven hours later, he reached the bottom of the mountain, hungry and exhausted.

As he limped into the parking lot, a group of rescue workers looked up in amazement and burst into cheers. "It's a miracle that he survived," one rescue worker said. "Usually we just find a body. This is the first time we've seen a person come out alive." When his friend Luc saw Joel, he began to cry with relief. "It was incredible," he said. "I was sure he wouldn't make it." Joel felt the candy bar wrapper in his pocket and remembered the name—Avalanche. "I was really lucky. I'm going to be more careful in the future," he said.

What are Joel's and Luc's future plans? They are already thinking about their next hikes. Luc wants to climb in Mexico with his girlfriend. For the moment, Joel is recovering from a broken ankle. But he has plans. He wants to climb Mont Blanc in France. He's just waiting until he can walk again.

Reading Skills

READING COMPREHENSION

Put the events in the correct order.

_____ Joel slid down the mountain and was buried in snow.

_____ The wind began to blow hard as the weather changed.

__1__ Joel and Luc bought snacks for their hike in the White Mountains.

_____ Luc arrived at the bottom of the mountain alone.

_____ The two friends were enjoying a routine Sunday hike.

_____ Joel used his ice ax to dig himself out of the snow.

_____ Rescue workers cheered when they saw Joel in the parking lot.

_____ Joel lost his footing and felt himself beginning to fall.

_____ Joel and Luc waited for morning.

_____ Joel managed to reach the parking lot with a broken ankle.

REVIEW THE VOCABULARY

Complete each sentence with a word from the list.

shelter
~~cave~~
exhausted
cheers
wrapper
place
blow
alive
relief
hike

1. Joel made a snow _____*cave*_____ and waited until morning.

2. Joel and Luc were enjoying a routine _____ in the mountains.

3. Suddenly, the wind began to _____ really hard.

4. Joel put his foot in the wrong _____ and began to fall.

5. The two men found _____ for the night.

6. Luc didn't know if Joel was _____.

7. The people who saw Joel burst into _____.

8. When he reached the bottom of the mountain, Joel was hungry and _____.

9. Luc began to cry with _____ when he saw his friend.

10. Joel could feel a candy bar _____ in his pocket.

RECYCLE THE VOCABULARY

Complete each sentence with the name of a body part from the list below.

waists
hand
arm
chin
ankle
foot
wrist
~~eyes~~

1. The volunteers couldn't believe their _____*eyes*_____.

2. The hikers were sinking in snow up to their _____.

3. Joel put his _____ in the wrong place.

4. Joel's right _____ was free of the snow.

5. Joel was buried up to his _____.

6. Joel's ice ax was attached to his _____.

7. Joel didn't realize that he had broken his _____.

8. Joel felt the candy bar wrapper with his _____.

Put It Together

Match each noun on the list with the adjective that describes it.

situation
lot
bar
~~facilities~~
drill
climber
wind
worker
ankle
shop

1. medical __facilities__

2. parking _____

3. snack _____

4. howling _____

5. mountain _____

6. rescue _____

7. broken _____

8. repair _____

9. power _____

10. life and death _____

Discuss these questions in groups.

1. What are some life and death situations?
2. Whom can you call in case of emergency? Make a list.
3. Do you know anyone who has saved a life? What happened?
4. What can people do to protect themselves from extreme heat or cold?
5. How can you learn more about what to do in an emergency?

TELL THE STORIES

A. In groups, act out the story "How a Power Drill Saved a Life."
You will need:

- three doctors: two in the north, one in a large city hospital
- a patient
- one or two nurses

Practice your roles. Then act out the story for another group or for the class.

B. In pairs, tell the story "He's Alive!" One person takes the role of Joel and the other takes the role of Luc. Each person describes what happened to him and how he felt during the avalanche and afterward.

WRITING OPTION

Imagine you are recovering from surgery in a clinic in an Arctic village. You find out that your doctors saved your life by using a power drill to operate on you. Write a letter to the doctors to thank them for saving your life. Ask them to tell you what happened.

BEYOND THE STORIES

Look for a story in the newspaper about an emergency situation or rescue. Bring the story to class. Explain what happened.

The Wave of the Future

STORY 1 X-SPORTS

STORY 2 PAGE ME!

Let's Get Ready

A. In each group, cross out the word or expression that doesn't belong.

to call	trendy	daredevil	fresh	boring
~~to sell~~	the rage	risky	new	exciting
to page	popular	strong	the future	risky
to telephone	expensive	close to the edge	competition	thrilling

B. Are these words synonyms or antonyms? Write S for synonym or A for antonym.

1. skintight   baggy   <u>A</u>   4. skill   ability   _____

2. steep   flat   _____   5. huge   small   _____

3. appeal   attraction   _____   6. trendy   popular   _____

15

Before You Read

A. Work in groups. Look at the list of sports below. Rate the sports according to danger and excitement on a scale of 1 to 10. No. 1 is most dangerous or most exciting. Complete the chart.

	Dangerous	Exciting
skiing		
golf		
wind surfing		
bungy jumping		
white-water rafting		
snowboarding		
hockey		
basketball		
mountain climbing		
mountain biking		

X-Sports

Rick Stevenson, 16 years old, spends every minute he can on the mountain. He and his friends go snowboarding every weekend. "It's incredible," he says. "The winds are so strong, the boards go 50 miles an hour." His friend Laura Fields agrees. "No one goes skiing anymore," she says. "That's for the old folks."

Rick and Laura are part of a new trend in sports. It has its own language, words such as "rage," "juice," and "energy." It has its own clothing, such as skin-tight bicycle suits in rainbow colors or baggy tops and pants. And it's not for the old or the easily frightened. Its philosophy is to get as close to the edge as possible. And more and more young athletes are taking part in these risky, daredevil activities called "extreme sports," or "X-sports."

In the past, young athletes would play hockey or baseball. Today, they want risk and excitement—the closer to the edge the better. They snowboard over cliffs and mountain-bike down steep mountains. They wind-surf near hurricanes, go white-water rafting through rapids, and bungy-jump from towers.

Extreme sports started as an alternative to more expensive sports. A city kid who didn't have the money to buy expensive sports equipment could get a skateboard and have fun. But now it has become a whole new area of sports, with specialized equipment and high levels of skill. There's even a special Olympics for extreme sports, called the Winter X-Games, which includes snow mountain biking and ice climbing. An Extreme Games competition is held each summer in Rhode Island. It features sports such as sky surfing, where people jump from airplanes with surfboards attached to their feet.

What makes extreme sports so popular? "People love the thrill," says Murray Nussbaum, who sells sports equipment. "City people want to be outdoors on the week-end and do something challenging. The new equipment is so much better that people can take more risks without getting hurt." An athlete adds, "Sure there's a risk, but that's part of the appeal. Once you go mountain biking or snow-boarding, it's impossible to go back to bike riding or skiing. It's just too boring."

Now even the older crowd is starting to join in. Every weekend a group of friends in their early 30s get together. During the week they work as computer programmers in the same office. On Sundays they rent mountain bikes that cost $2,000 each and ride down steep mountains together.

Extreme sports are certainly not for everyone. Most people still prefer to play baseball or basketball or watch sports on TV. But extreme sports are definitely gaining in popularity. "These sports are fresh and exciting. It's the wave of the future. The potential is huge," says Nussbaum.

Reading Skills

FOCUS ON THE EXACT INFORMATION

Answer the questions with exact information from the story. Use the number of words suggested.

1. What does Laura Fields say about going skiing these days? (5 words)

   _____ That's for the old folks. _____

2. Give examples of new sports terms. (3 words)

   _____

3. What's the philosophy of the new sports trend? (5 words)

   Get as close _____.

4. What does "X-Sports" mean? (2 words)

   It means _____.

5. What do young people want today? (2 words)

   They want _____ and _____.

6. What were extreme sports an alternative to? (3 words)

   They started as an alternative to _____.

7. What do people love about extreme sports? (1 word)

   They love the _____.

8. What does one athlete say about risk? (2 words)

   It's part of _____.

9. How do people who practice extreme sports find regular sports? (1 word)

They find them _____.

10. What does Murray Nussbaum say about extreme sports? (2 words)

The _____ is _____.

REVIEW THE VOCABULARY

Complete each expression with the correct preposition from the list.

from
of
down
over
to
~~without~~
up
in

1. taking risks ____without____ getting hurt

2. a new trend _____ sports

3. as close _____ the edge as possible

4. snowboarding _____ the edge of cliffs

5. mountain biking _____ steep mountains

6. climbing _____ icy mountains

7. bungy jumping _____ towers

8. the wave _____ the future

BUILD YOUR VOCABULARY

Underline the correct words to complete the paragraph.

Extreme sports are all the rage. It's not for the old or easily
(1. <u>frightened</u>, tired, young). The idea is to get as close to the
(2. place, edge, sport) as possible. Athletes like the (3. time, risk,
space) and excitement. Extreme sports are an (4. energy, activity, alternative) to other sports, which some people now find
(5. bored, scared, boring). X-sports use specialized (6. equipment,
ideas, area) and require high levels of (7. money, thrills, skill).
They're very popular with young people, who love the (8. mountains, crowds, challenge). On weekends, friends get together to
(9. rent, buy, watch) mountain bikes and (10. leave, run, ride)
down steep mountains. Extreme sports aren't for everyone, but
they are definitely the wave of the future.

Before You Read

A. Discuss these questions in groups.

1. How much time do you spend on the phone every day?
2. Whom do you speak to most often?
3. What is the average length of your calls?
4. What is the longest phone call you ever made?
5. Whom was it to?

B. How do you communicate with the people in your life? Check the ways that apply to you. Compare your charts in groups.

	Write Letters	Phone	Fax	E-mail	Use a Pager
your best friend					
family members					
acquaintances					
relatives					
classmates					
employers					
co-workers					

Page Me !

A. When 15-year-old high school student Andrea Berish wants to send her friends a message, she doesn't call them on the phone. She uses a code that looks something like this: 90*401773. And she uses the latest technology to catch on with teenagers—pagers.

B. For many years, pagers (also called beepers) were used mainly by doctors and other professionals who had to be in constant contact with their work. More recently, working parents started buying pagers to keep in touch with their families. Parents began giving them to their teenagers when their sons or daughters went out on dates in the evenings. Now pagers have become all the rage with teenagers. They use them to keep in touch with friends and family, and they are developing new languages and codes to communicate.

C. The codes are a mixture of phrases and expressions. Some teens carry around sheets of paper with information to help them decode the messages. Some of the codes are private or use local expressions. But other codes are becoming well known across the country. For example, the code 90*401773 means "go home." Andrea explains: "The number 9 looks like the letter g. Zeros are Os. That part's easy. The number 4 looks like the letter H without legs.

The number 1 next to two 7s looks like the letter M. And the number 3 looks like the letter E backwards."

D. The codes aren't only in English. Julia Rodrigues, an 18-year-old student, often pages her friends and her boyfriend in Spanish. She signs her messages with the numbers 83505, which looks like the word *besos*, Spanish for *kisses*. "That's how they know who's calling," she says.

E. Teenagers have made pagers part of their culture in more ways than one. Because teens are the fastest-growing market for these devices, manufacturers have developed pagers that appeal to them. "Once, pagers were black and looked functional," says a manufacturer. "Now they come in many colors. Some have baseball or hockey logos on them. We even have fluorescent, glow-in-the-dark, and transparent pagers. They're very trendy." Pagers are also popular with teenagers because they're inexpensive to use. Pagers can start at about $30, with service charges of about $8 per month.

F. Many different companies are getting in on the deals. One company has an information network that communicates through pagers. Another company markets a pager that can translate many of the codes into language. And it provides new codes for phrases like "Let's play golf," in the hopes of attracting older customers.

G. But at the moment teenagers are the biggest buyers of pagers. Andrea says, "They're really cool. I was so excited when I got my pager." She remembers the first time she got a call on her pager. "I was sitting in school. My pager was attached to my belt. All of a sudden I felt it vibrate, and I sat up straight in class. My teacher said, 'Andrea, do you have an answer?' I said, 'No, I just got paged!'"

Reading Skills

Complete each sentence below with detailed information from the story. Look back at the story to find the answers.

1. ___Fifteen-year-old high school student Andrea Berish___ sends her friends messages by pager.

2. _____ were the main users of pagers for many years.

3. _____ started buying pagers to stay in touch with their families.

4. _____ are developing languages and codes for pagers.

5. _____ are mixtures of phrases and expressions.

6. _____ pages her friends in Spanish.

7. _____ know who's calling when the message is 83505.

8. _____ have developed colored and fluo-rescent pagers.

9. _____ cost about $8 a month.

10. _____ could be attracted by a "Let's play golf" code.

REVIEW THE EXPRESSIONS

Match the words with the expressions that have similar meanings.

translate into language	1. to market _____to sell_____
telephone	2. beeper _____
~~to sell~~	3. catch on _____
pager	4. get in touch _____
the newest	5. all the rage _____
become popular	6. the latest _____
contact	7. decode _____
very trendy	8. inexpensive _____
cheap	9. get in on _____
be part of	10. to call _____

USE THE CONTEXT TO FIND THE MEANING

Sometimes pronouns and other words are used to hold a story to-gether. It is important to know exactly what these words refer to. Use the context to find the meaning of the underlined words be-low. Then write the words or ideas they refer to on the lines.

1. Paragraph A: . . . she doesn't call <u>them</u> . . . ____her friends____

2. Paragraph B: . . . Parents began giving <u>them</u> . . .

   _____

3. Paragraph B: <u>They</u> use them to keep in touch. . . .

   _____

4. Paragraph C: . . . to help <u>them</u> decode . . . _____

5. Paragraph D: That's how <u>they</u> know who's calling.

   _____

6. Paragraph E: . . . market for <u>these devices</u> . . . _____

7. Paragraph E: Now <u>they</u> come in many colors._____

8. Paragraph E: <u>They</u>'re very trendy. _____

_____

9. Paragraph F: And <u>it</u> provides new codes . . . _____

10. Paragraph G: . . . I felt <u>it</u> vibrate . . . _____

Put It Together

LET'S REVIEW

The word **because** *shows the cause of an action or situation.*
Match the effects in List A with the causes in List B.

List A

1. Extreme sports are popular with

   young people __*e*__

2. Andrea sat up straight in class _____

3. Extreme sports need high levels of

   skill _____

4. Manufacturers have pagers in many

   colors _____

5. Some teens carry around sheets of

   paper _____

6. People can take more risks _____

7. Pagers are popular with teenagers

   _____

8. People don't go back to skiing _____

List B

a. because they can be dangerous.

b. because they are inexpensive.

c. because she was paged.

d. because they want to decode the messages.

e. because they like the thrill.

f. because it's too boring.

g. because the new equipment is much better.

h. because teenagers are a fast-growing market.

TALK ABOUT IT

Discuss these questions in groups.

1. Why do people participate in risky sports?
2. What is the riskiest thing you have ever done?
3. Do teenagers take more risks than adults? Explain.
4. Why do you think pagers are so popular with teenagers now?
5. Do you know anyone who has a pager? Why does that person have it?
6. Would you like to have a pager? Why or why not?

TELL THE STORIES

A. Tell the story "X-Sports." Imagine you are a teenager who loves to participate in extreme sports. Explain to an older person:

- which sport you chose
- what you wear
- how you do it
- the risks involved
- why you like it

B. Act out the story "Page Me!" One person takes the role of a teenager. The other person takes the role of his or her parent. The teenager tries to convince the parent that he or she needs a pager, using the arguments from the story and any others he or she can think of.

WRITING OPTION

Imagine you are a teenager and you want your parents to buy you a pager. Write a letter to your parents, convincing them to get you a pager. Explain how all your friends have pagers and that you need to be able to communicate with them.

BEYOND THE STORIES

A. Go to a sports shop in your neighborhood. Find out about the equipment needed to play any of the extreme sports mentioned in the story.

or

Go to a shop that sells telephones and pagers. Find out about the pagers that are available and their costs.

Share your information in the next class.

B. Look in the newspaper for a sports story about an extreme sport. Bring the article to class. Be prepared to discuss the story and give information about the sport.

Looking Good

STORY 1   THE MOST BEAUTIFUL WOMEN
IN THE WORLD

STORY 2   GETTING PIERCED

Let's Get Ready

Match the questions to the answers.

1. Which word means <u>put a needle through something</u>? <u>*e*</u>

2. Which word means <u>eat less to lose weight</u>? ____

3. What word describes an important job? ____

4. Which part of the body is between the ear and the nose? ____

5. What does <u>take a leave of absence</u> mean? ____

6. Where is Venezuela? ____

7. What can people with crooked teeth do? ____

8. What part of the body do people in India pierce? ____

9. Which part of the body is in the mouth? ____

10. What do some people put on their faces? ____

11. What do people do before they exercise? ____

12. What is a <u>sponsor</u>? ____

a. the nose

b. stop work temporarily

c. stretch their bodies

d. the cheek

e. pierce

f. the tongue

g. makeup

h. straighten them

i. someone who pays for something

j. in South America

k. diet

l. mayor

THE MOST BEAUTIFUL WOMEN IN THE WORLD

Before You Read

A. Discuss these questions in groups.

1. What kind of beauty contests do you know about?

2. Who participates in them?

3. What do the contestants do?

4. Are beauty contests a good idea? Why or why not?

B. Work with a partner. Talk about the connotations of the words below. Put a check mark (✓) in the correct places.

	Positive	Negative
effort	✓	
pride		
silly		
honored		
admire		
winner		
sacrifice		
fortunately		
starve		
obsession		
advantage		
opportunity		

The Most Beautiful Women in the World

A. Who are the most beautiful women in the world? Looking at the records, people might think Venezuelan women are. They win the Miss Latin America, Miss Universe, and Miss World contests more frequently than women from any other country. In Venezuela, the term "Miss," as in "Miss Universe," is an honored title.

B. These days, people in some cultures consider beauty contests to be silly. They have tried to stop these contests, saying the contests treat women as objects and place too much importance on women's looks. But in Latin America, beauty contests are a source of pride. And in Venezuela, they are almost a national obsession.

C. Are Venezuelan women really more beautiful than other women? "They are not really more beautiful here," says Selena, who trains girls for the contest. "It's just that the girls here work harder and prepare more than anyone else." Preparing for a contest is a full-time job that involves sixteen-hour-days for six months. Many of the women take a leave of absence from their jobs during the training period. "If you don't take this seriously, you don't have a chance," Selena says.

D. The preparation takes many hours a day. The contestants stretch their bodies and practice their walks down the runway. They work on their speeches and practice answering questions such as, "Whom do you admire most in the world?" They starve to stay slim. They take classes to learn how to style their hair and apply makeup. Most of them grow their hair long and diet to lose at least 10 pounds. Many of them have their teeth straightened or undergo plastic surgery to straighten noses or fix other body parts.

E. It isn't easy, and the contestants sacrifice a lot for the contest. One Miss Universe winner immediately put on 20 pounds after the contest. She said the only thing she wanted to do after the contest was to eat. The financial cost is high as well. The training for the Miss Venezuela and Miss Universe contests can cost up to $60,000. Fortunately the television station that sponsors the contest pays the costs of grooming the finalists.

F. Yet most of the contestants say it's worth the effort. A former Miss Universe is now mayor of a district in a large city. Although she had no political experience before that, she has been asked to run for higher political office. Another winner has her own television show. Winners have an advantage they could not get anywhere else. "It's the only chance you have to make it," says one contestant. "You can't get these opportunities any other way."

Reading Skills

READ FOR THE MAIN IDEAS

Write the letter of the paragraph that is mainly about each of the following topics.

1. opinions about contests _B_

2. difficulties for contestants _____

3. Selena's comments _____

4. training for the contest _____

5. Venezuelan women _____

6. benefits for contestants _____

Circle the letter of the correct completion for each sentence.

1. Venezuelan women win beauty contests
   a. about as often as women from other countries.
   (b.) more often than women from other countries.
   c. less often than women from other countries.

2. Some cultures consider beauty contests silly because
   a. women spend too much time preparing for them.
   b. they think the contests place too much importance on looks.
   c. they think the contests make women look too important.

3. When they prepare for a contest, Venezuelan women
   a. work harder than other women.
   b. get full-time jobs.
   c. don't take the contest seriously.

4. One thing a woman may do to prepare for a contest is
   a. straighten her teeth.
   b. cut her hair.
   c. talk to people she admires.

5. A Miss Universe contestant gained weight after the contest because
   a. there was a big party after the contest.
   b. she wanted to gain 20 pounds.
   c. she was always hungry during the contest.

6. A former Miss Universe who is now mayor of a district
   a. may run for higher political office.
   b. has a lot of political experience.
   c. wants to move to a larger city.

BUILD YOUR VOCABULARY

Match the things the beauty contestants do, according to the story.

1. starve __i__
2. style ____
3. practice ____
4. apply ____
5. undergo ____
6. run ____
7. fix ____
8. pay ____
9. lose ____
10. stretch ____
11. prepare ____
12. straighten ____

a. their walks
b. the costs
c. their hair
d. 10 pounds
e. body parts
f. plastic surgery
g. makeup
h. for many hours
i. to stay slim
j. their bodies
k. for political office
l. their teeth

UNDERSTAND FACT AND OPINION

A fact is something you can see or prove. An opinion is what someone thinks or believes. Read these sentences with a partner. Decide if the information is a fact or an opinion. Write F for **fact** *or O for* **opinion.**

1. The most beautiful women in the world are from Venezuela.

   _O_

2. Venezuelan women win more beauty contests than women from other countries. _____

3. Beauty contests are silly and treat women as objects. _____

4. For a young woman, entering a beauty contest is worth the effort. _____

5. Some women take leaves of absence from their jobs to prepare for beauty contests. _____

6. Plastic surgery is necessary to win a beauty contest. _____

7. Many contestants diet to lose weight. _____

8. One Miss Universe put on 20 pounds when the contest was over. _____

9. Beauty contest winners have advantages they can't get anywhere else. _____

10. Winning the Miss Universe contest is a great honor. _____

RECYCLE THE VOCABULARY

Work with a partner to complete the crossword puzzle. Look back at the story to help you.

Across

2. another word for <u>give up</u> (paragraph E)

4. what people think Venezuelan women are (paragraph A)

5. something contestants do to help their bodies move more easily (paragraph D)

6. what beauty contests mean to South Americans and Latin Americans (paragraph B)

8. People take a leave of _____ from work. (paragraph C)

10. When you don't eat, you _____. (paragraph D)

12. something contestants get from the contests (paragraph F)

13. what people do to lose weight (paragraph D)

14. a kind of surgery (paragraph D)

Down

1. often (paragraph A)

2. Some people think beauty contests are _____. (paragraph B)

3. right away (paragraph E)

7. energy and sacrifice (paragraph F)

9. what some contestants do to their teeth (paragraph D)

11. "Miss Universe" is an honored _____ (paragraph A)

12. a very strong interest in something (paragraph B)

Before You Read

Discuss these questions in groups.

1. What are some ways people decorate their bodies?
2. Why do people pierce their bodies?
3. Who are most likely to get parts of their bodies pierced?
4. What parts of their bodies do people often pierce?
5. How do you think it feels to get pierced?
6. Are there any dangers connected with getting pierced? Explain.

Getting Pierced

When Melanie and Sacha fell in love, they decided to do something together. They got their tongues pierced. "One day I just decided to do it," says 24-year-old Melanie. Together, Melanie and Sacha went to the Black Sun Studio. Sacha went first. He held out his tongue for Pierre Black, the studio owner. Pierre quickly pushed a needle, followed by the jewelry, through Sacha's tongue. Then Pierre repeated the procedure for Melanie. When it was over, the couple kissed. "I feel great," says Melanie. "Me too. A little sore, but happy," says Sacha. "I feel like we bonded."

Why did they do it? People often associate body piercing with street kids who have safety pins all over their faces. But that's only a small part of it. Pierre says, "People pierce their bodies for all kinds of reasons. They pierce to mark their independence when they move out on their own. Couples get pierced to show their commitment to each other. There are a lot of different reasons why people do it. You'd be surprised who comes in for body piercing."

People have pierced and decorated their bodies throughout history. Ear piercing has been popular in Europe since the eighteenth century, when rich women wore diamonds in their ears to show their wealth. People in India have been piercing their noses for a long time. Group members often show they belong by piercing certain body parts. And some cultures consider it beautiful to push needles through the skin. "Body piercing has been practiced everywhere. It's a personal statement that people use to show their individuality," says Pierre. "Every culture has its own idea of beauty, and people use body piercing, just like hairstyles or clothes, to express themselves."

Pierre began piercing seven years ago. He studied anatomy books and consulted doctors to find out the best way to pierce the skin. He read anthropology books to learn how piercing is done in other cultures. And he learned from experienced piercers. He says he has probably pierced almost every part of the human body. Recently the most popular part is the navel, but Pierre has pierced noses, lips, cheeks, elbows, tongues, eyebrows, and even the web between the thumb and the forefinger.

Pierre insists that body piercing is safe if it's done properly, but he warns people to be careful. The industry isn't regulated, and anyone can set up shop. "Some shops are dirty. It's important to make sure the place is clean," he says. He suggests that people ask around for recommendations. There are good and bad places, just as in any other industry. He admits there can be health risks but says, "Peo-

ple have been piercing for centuries without any problems. You just have to be careful who you go to."

Pierre remembers one customer clearly. A young woman came to him after she tried to commit suicide. She wanted to be pierced to show her commitment to life. "Some people pierce for physical reasons, others for spiritual reasons. People have a lot of ways to show their individuality. Body piercing is one way to express who you are."

Reading Skills

READING COMPREHENSION

Read the sentences and write **T** *for* **true** *or* **F** *for* **false** *according to the information in the story.*

1. Melanie and Sacha pierced their tongues to show commitment to each other. __T__

2. People often think of street kids when they talk about body piercing. ____

3. Most people get pierced to show they are different. ____

4. People started to pierce their bodies about 100 years ago. ____

5. Piercing is often cultural. ____

6. Most cultures have similar ideas about beauty. ____

7. Pierre studied piercing at a special school. ____

8. Lips are the most popular body part for piercing today. ____

9. According to Pierre, piercing is safe if it is done properly. ____

10. Most places that do body piercing are regulated. ____

11. Some people pierce their bodies for spiritual reasons. ____

12. Pierre says that people pierce to express themselves. ____

SCAN FOR THE DETAILS

Write the name of the person or people for each of the following.

1. _Melanie and Sacha_ decided to have their tongues pierced.

2. _____ owns the Black Star Studio.

3. _____ kissed Melanie after they got pierced.

4. _____ get pierced to show commitment.

5. _____ wore diamonds in their ears in Europe.

6. _____ have pierced their noses for a long time.

7. _____ show they belong by getting pierced.

8. _____ studied anatomy books.

9. _____ tried to commit suicide.

10. _____ get pierced for spiritual reasons.

REVIEW THE VOCABULARY

Label the diagram with the body parts mentioned in the text.

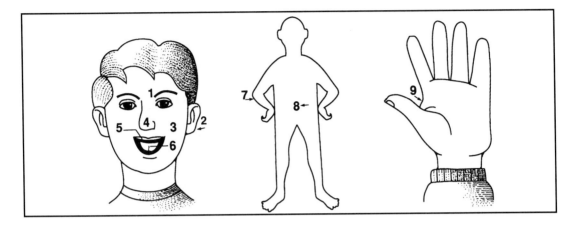

eyebrow __1__   navel ____   web between thumb

tongue ____   lip ____   and forefinger____

nose ____   cheek ____

ear ____   elbow ____

SKIM TO CHECK THE INFORMATION

Skim the story. Which reasons are given for body piercing?

1. to feel bonded ✔

2. to annoy parents ____

3. to mark independence ____

4. to show commitment ____

5. to attract attention ____

6. to impress friends ____

7. to show wealth ____

8. to show belonging ____

9. to be beautiful ____

10. to show individuality ____

11. to improve health ____

12. to show commitment for

    life ____

13. to win a bet ____

14. to express who you are ____

15. for spiritual reasons ____

Put It Together

Make six sentences using the words from Lists A, B, and C.

List A	List B	List C
1. ~~Some cultures consider~~	is a full-time job	if done properly
	body piercing is safe	to each other
2. Preparing for beauty contests	body piercing	for the contests
3. Many people associate	to show their commitment	with street kids
4. Pierre insists that	time and money	for six months
5. Couples get pierced	~~beauty contests~~	~~to be silly~~
6. The beauty contestants sacrifice		

1. _____ Some cultures consider beauty contests to be silly _____.

2. _____.

3. _____.

4. _____.

5. _____.

6. _____.

1. What is your idea of beauty?

2. What kinds of things do women and men in your culture do to make themselves attractive?

3. Is there any value to beauty contests? Explain.

4. Do you think body piercing and tattoos are attractive? Explain why or why not.

5. Who do you think are the most attractive man and woman in the world today? Explain your answer.

TELL THE STORIES

A. Tell the story "The Most Beautiful Women in the World." Imagine you are a reporter who is covering the Miss Universe contest. Explain how Venezuelan women frequently win the title and why you think this happens. Give some background about how Venezuelan women prepare for the contest.

B. Tell the story "Getting Pierced." Imagine you are Pierre Black and have a body piercing studio. A young man or woman comes to you to get pierced but hesitates about going ahead. Explain:

- the background of body piercing
- how you learned the trade
- different reasons why people pierce their bodies
- why your shop is a good place to get it done

WRITING OPTION

Write a composition in which you agree or disagree with this statement about beauty contests: "Beauty contests are silly and treat women as objects."

BEYOND THE STORIES

Look in the yellow pages of your telephone directory or in the classified ads in your newspaper. See if you can find any ads for body piercing. Bring any ads you find to class and discuss what you found. What information is given in the ads? Would you go to these places? Why or why not?

UNIT 4

Outer Space

STORY 1   CRUMBS FROM HEAVEN

STORY 2   WHO'S OUT THERE?

Let's Get Ready

A. Match the words to the definitions.

1. alien ___i___   a. a creature

2. meteorite _____   b. place where aircraft land

3. abducted _____   c. small pieces of something

4. flying saucer _____   d. a story told to hide the true facts

5. landing site _____   e. stone or metal from outer space

6. myth _____   f. thing or things

7. a cover-up _____   g. public sale

8. stuff _____   h. story not based on facts

9. a being _____   i. person from a different place

10. granules _____   j. taken away or kidnapped

11. auction _____   k. a person who doubts or questions

12. skeptic _____   l. spaceship

B. What do you know about outer space? Look at the list below. In groups, talk about any information you have about these things.

- UFOs

- Roswell, New Mexico

- aliens from other planets

- meteorites

- spaceships

- alien-based movies

- life on Mars

- Pathfinder

- life on other planets

Before You Read

Complete the chart by putting these words into categories. Some words may belong in both categories.

	Large	Small
spaceship	✓	
speck		
dust		
rock		
trinket		
planet		
meteor		
heaven		
slice		
pebble		
crumb		
particle		
desert		

Crumbs from Heaven

"This ugly black stuff may look like a rock from your garden," says Frank McDermott, "but it's worth a lot of money. When it comes to stuff from space, *the sky's the limit*, as they say."

Frank McDermott used to dig for gold. Now he looks up at the sky to see what's there. He knows that anything that comes from the sky is worth a lot of money. And the prices are going up. At one point, a 16-inch meteorite found in the African desert in 1936 sold for $2,000. Three years later, it sold at an auction for $40,000. Americans are developing meteor mania. They want any kind of material that comes from the sky, and they are willing to pay for it.

When the Pathfinder spaceship returned from Mars with reports of primitive life on the planet, the frenzy began. Only twelve meteors have come from Mars, and they sell for more than $1,000 a gram. On one home shopping channel, 4,000 viewers each paid $90 for a speck of a meteorite from Mars. They received granules of the meteorite in a plastic tube. "It was so cool to watch those pictures of Mars," says Joyce Brooks, an avid collector. "I was so happy to get anything from another planet, even a small pebble. I have a special place for it on my bookcase."

"People are becoming obsessed with this stuff," says Henry Cullen, who owns a store that sells rocks and gems. "They're crazy about anything from another world." A small piece of meteorite at Cullen's store sells for about $60. A larger slice of the rock can easily sell for $2,000 or more. Cullen says some people are buying pieces of meteorites for investment. They think they will outperform the stock market. "I sold $30,000 worth of meteorites to investors last year. I tell them it's a great investment," Cullen says.

Now some scientists say they can't get hold of the meteorites they need to do research because dealers can sell them to collectors for large sums of money. "There's too much competition. We can hardly afford to buy them any-more," says a research scientist. "It's awful that people are cutting up the meteorites to make earrings and trinkets. Meteorites are complex things. You have to study the whole object. You can't just break off pieces."

But Cullen disagrees. He says that meteorites can be cut up without losing any scientific value. He spent months figuring out how to market a piece of meteorite. First he ground it to dust, but he lost thousands of dollars. Finally he found a way to put the particles into plastic cubes. "I know this looks like rocks from a driveway," he says, "but everyone wants something from heaven, even if it looks like crumbs."

Reading Skills

READING COMPREHENSION

Read the questions and write the answers.

1. What is the "ugly black stuff" that's worth a lot of money?

   <u>stuff from space</u>

2. How much did the price of the 16-inch meteorite increase in three years?

   _____

3. What is meteor mania?

_____

4. At what point did meteors from Mars suddenly become a craze?

_____

5. What inspired Joyce to want granules of a meteorite?

_____

6. What is the price range for pieces of meteorite in Henry Cullen's store?

_____

7. Why does Henry Cullen say some people invest in meteors?

_____

8. Why can't scientists get the meteorites they need anymore?

_____

9. Why don't scientists want meteorites to be cut up?

_____

10. How did Mr. Cullen make money from a piece of meteorite?

_____

SCAN FOR THE DETAILS

Write the name of the person or thing on each line.

1. <u>Anything that comes from the sky</u> is worth a lot of money.

2. _____ sold for $40,000.

3. Pathfinder is _____.

4. Meteors from Mars sell for _____.

5. _____ each paid

   $90 for a speck of a meteorite from Mars.

6. Henry Cullen's store sells _____.

7. Last year Mr. Cullen's sales to investors amounted to

   _____.

8. _____ can't afford

   to buy meteorites anymore.

9. People are making _____ out

   of meteorites.

10. Mr. Cullen describes the pieces of meteorite as

   _____.

VOCABULARY IN CONTEXT

Find the expressions in the story. Then use the context to find the phrase that has a similar meaning.

1. The sky's the limit.
   a. The sky is out of reach.
   (b.) Anything's possible.
2. Americans are developing meteor mania.
   a. Americans want to buy meteors.
   b. Americans want to travel to meteors.
3. The frenzy began.
   a. Things became chaotic.
   b. People had a lot of fun.
4. a home shopping channel
   a. gossip about good bargains
   b. a special television network

5. <u>granules</u> of the meteorite
   a. big pieces
   b. small pieces
6. It was so cool.
   a. The temperature dropped.
   b. It was exciting.
7. <u>outperforms</u> the stock market
   a. is more profitable than
   b. isn't as profitable as
8. can't get hold of
   a. isn't able to keep
   b. isn't able to find
9. earrings and <u>trinkets</u>
   a. expensive things
   b. inexpensive things
10. figuring out
   a. asking about
   b. deciding

DICTATION

Read this paragraph. Then close your book and write it as your teacher dictates it.

Planets and stars are not the only things in outer space. Meteorites are pieces of stone or metal from the sky that sometimes come to Earth. They come to Earth so quickly that they often burn up. When meteorites land on the Earth, people become very excited. It's a little like meeting a visitor from another planet.

Before You Read

Discuss these questions in groups. Explain your answers.

1. Do you think there is life on other planets?
2. Do you think aliens from other planets have visited Earth?
3. What do you think aliens look like?
4. How do you think aliens would communicate with people on Earth?
5. Do you think aliens are more intelligent than people on Earth?
6. Do you think aliens are friendly or dangerous?
7. Would you like to meet someone from another planet?
8. Would you like to travel to outer space? Where would you want to go?

Who's Out There?

Do you believe there's life in outer space? A recent poll asked 900 American adults this question. Sixty percent answered yes. Over 40 percent of the college graduates believe that flying saucers have visited the Earth. Close to 50 percent thought aliens were more intelligent than people on Earth. Eighty-five percent also said they thought aliens were friendly rather than hostile.

Many people are convinced that aliens visit us regularly. They say that the American government knows this but is covering it up. In the last few years, thousands of Americans say they have been abducted by aliens. In fact, there is

so much common knowledge about aliens that people can even describe what they look like: tall and slender, with huge heads and almond-shaped eyes. There are models of aliens in the UFO (unidentified flying object) Museum and Research Center in Roswell, New Mexico.

Roswell, New Mexico, is where it all started, over fifty years ago. In 1947, a farmer in the area found some strange, shiny material on the ground. He gave it to the sheriff, who turned it over to the army. The army sent out a press release about a "flying disk." The local newspaper made a slight change and wrote a story about a "flying saucer" in the

Roswell region. The next day, the army changed the story and said that the material was from a weather balloon. Everyone forgot about the incident for many years.

Then in the 1980s, several stories were published about the Roswell incident. Some people said that a spaceship had crashed on the farmland and that three to five alien bodies had been found. The bodies were being kept by the government in a secret place. The government denied the story, but many people didn't believe it. Seventy-one percent of the people polled said they believed the government knew more than they were telling people. "People would panic if they knew what really happened," said an observer.

Now Roswell has become a meeting place for people who believe in aliens. On the fiftieth anniversary of the rumors of a spaceship landing, more than 100,000 people gathered in the desert town, where the temperature can reach 110 degrees. They went out in the hot sun to look for the burn mark the spaceship left when it crashed against a rock. They paid $15 each for a viewing. No one complained when they didn't see a spaceship. They were just happy to be there.

Why all the interest in aliens? People are worried about problems on Earth and are suspicious of new technologies. Perhaps this leads them to believe there are beings who are more intelligent than we are. They hope these beings will save us and teach us better ways to live.

Of course, a lot of people are making money on these beliefs. Motel owners in Roswell say a quarter of their visitors come to see the alien landing site. Stores in Roswell sell everything from stuffed alien dolls to alien refrigerator magnets. The media play up the belief as well. Alien-based movies and television shows feature government cover-ups and alien invasions. And the fourth most popular talk show in America is about UFOs and aliens.

Skeptics say this is all a myth. People want to believe we are not alone in the universe, but no facts prove there is life anywhere else. Others disagree. "We just don't know if aliens exist," says a researcher. "But technology changes so quickly. Years ago people would never believe some of the things we can do today. Who knows what's out there? We have to keep looking."

Reading Skills

SKIM TO CHECK THE INFORMATION

Half of the sentences below are true according to the story. The other sentences have incorrect information. Write **T** *for* **true** *and* **F** *for* **false**. *Correct the wrong information.*

1. A majority of Americans believe there is life in outer space.

   __T__

2. Many people believe the U.S. government is hiding information about aliens. ____

3. Everyone has a different idea of an alien's physical appearance.

   ____

4. At first, people thought the shiny material in Roswell was from a weather balloon. ____

5. People think the government is hiding the bodies of aliens.

   ____

6. People say a spaceship crashed into a rock in New Mexico.

   ____

7. People who didn't see the spaceship were disappointed. ____

8. The majority of people who stay in Roswell motels come to see alien landing sites. ____

9. There is a popular talk show devoted to aliens and UFOs. ____

10. Serious people all agree that aliens don't exist. ____

UNDERSTAND THE MAIN IDEAS AND DETAILS

*You can understand a story more clearly if you group main ideas
with the details and the examples that support them. Choose the
main ideas from the list and write them in the first column in the
"Notes" table to match the details in the second column. The first
main idea is put in for you.*

Main ideas

rumors that began in 1947

gathering in Roswell, New Mexico

a survey about life in outer space

new rumors in the 1980s

people making money from alien stories

~~beliefs about aliens~~

Notes

Main ideas	Details
beliefs about aliens	- U.S. government cover-up
	- abductions by aliens
	- tall, slender, big heads, almond-eyed
_____	- 60% believe in life in outer space
	- 40% of college students believe in UFOs
	- 50% believe aliens are more intelligent
	- 85% say aliens are friendly

_____ - shiny material on farm

- army press release

- newspaper story about flying saucer

- army changes story

_____ - spaceship crashed

- alien bodies found

- 71% believe government cover-up

_____ - fiftieth anniversary celebration of landing

- 100,000 people come to Roswell

- $15 to see rock hit by spaceship

_____ - visits to alien landing sites

- alien dolls and refrigerator magnets

- alien-based movies popular

- popular radio talk show about aliens

READING COMPREHENSION

Put the events of the Roswell story in the correct order.

_____ The army changed its story and said the shiny material was from a weather balloon.

_____ The government denied the story about alien bodies.

_____ The sheriff gave the material to the army.

_____ Rumors about alien bodies being stored by the government began to circulate.

_____ The local newspaper wrote about a "flying saucer."

__1__ A farmer near Roswell found some shiny material on the ground.

_____ The farmer gave the material to the sheriff.

_____ Several stories were published about Roswell.

_____ The army sent out a press release about a "flying disk."

_____ One hundred thousand people gathered for the fiftieth anniversary of the UFO landing.

SCAN FOR THE DETAILS

Answer the questions using numbers from the flying saucer. Add these symbols where necessary: % ° th 's

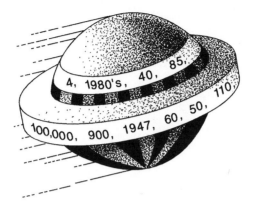

1. What percentage of Americans polled think there is life in outer space? _60%_

2. When did alien stories start? _____

3. When were stories about Roswell published? _____

4. How many people went to the fiftieth anniversary? _____

5. How hot was it in Roswell? _____

6. What is the ranking of the talk show about UFOs? _____

7. What was the number of Americans polled? _____

8. What percentage of the college graduates polled think flying saucers have visited Earth? _____

9. What percentage of the people polled think aliens are more intelligent than we are? _____

10. What percentage of the people polled think aliens are friendly? _____

Put It Together

Check the words that apply according to information from the stories.

1. Eight beliefs about aliens

   ✓ tall

   ____ slender

   ____ green

   ____ friendly

   ____ from Mars

   ____ visit regularly

   ____ huge heads

   ____ hostile

   ____ intelligent

   ____ almond-shaped eyes

   ____ come in spaceships

   ____ speak English

2. Nine things that describe meteorites

   ____ look like rocks

   ____ found in African desert

   ____ are made of gold

   ____ come from Mars

   ____ sold in plastic cubes

   ____ black

   ____ are easy to find

   ____ are different colors

   ____ sell at auctions

   ____ are made into trinkets

   ____ are complex things

   ____ have gone up in price

3. Eight things people spend money on

_____ alien refrigerator magnets

_____ alien-based movies

_____ books about meteorites

_____ stuffed alien dolls

_____ building spaceships

_____ meteorites for investment

_____ viewing a spaceship landing site

_____ specks of meteorites

_____ special bookcases to hold meteorites

_____ meteorite jewelry and trinkets

_____ meteorite particles in cubes

_____ building homes on earth for aliens

TALK ABOUT IT

1. Why do you think people are so interested in outer space?

2. What movies or television shows have you seen about aliens?

3. How realistic do you think these shows are?

4. Do you think people on Earth will ever travel to distant planets? Explain.

TELL THE STORIES

A. Tell the story "Crumbs from Heaven." Imagine you own a store that sells rocks and gems and a customer comes in to ask about buying meteorite particles. Explain:

- why people are so interested in meteorites
- how you are selling the pieces of meteorite
- why the situation has changed over the years
- what you think of people collecting meteorites

B. Tell the story "Who's Out There?" in pairs. One person believes that aliens have visited the Earth. The other person doesn't believe in aliens. Present your arguments in front of the class or a small group of students. Use the information from the story and any other information you want to add.

WRITING OPTION

Imagine that you have just visited Roswell, New Mexico. Write a letter to a friend describing what you saw and giving your opinions about UFOs and aliens.

A. Look for information on aliens in the following places:

- a TV show
- a movie
- a radio show
- a newspaper or magazine story
- a book

In the next class explain what you saw or read and how realistic you think it is.

B. Do a survey. Ask five people outside of class these questions. Share your information in the next class.

1. Do you believe flying saucers and aliens from outer space have visited Earth?
2. Do you believe these aliens are more intelligent or less intelligent than people on Earth?
3. Do you think these aliens are friendly or hostile? Why?

A New Beginning

STORY 1   A LUCKY TIME TO GET MARRIED

STORY 2   CREATING HARMONY

Let's Get Ready

What do you know about customs in different cultures? Work in groups. Circle the letter of the best answer to each question.

1. What is the most popular month for weddings in North America?
   a. May
   b. June
   c. July

2. In which country is May 18 a lucky day to get married?
   a. the United States
   b. Malaysia
   c. China

3. What is smudging?
   a. a teenage dating custom
   b. a ritual to chase away spirits
   c. a wedding ritual

4. Who are <u>bridesmaids</u>?

    a. female household workers

    b. women who are married

    c. friends of the bride

5. What is <u>chanting</u>?

    a. repeating words over and over

    b. a kind of popular music

    c. a kind of dance

6. Which thing would a spiritualist do?

    a. perform a wedding ceremony

    b. be around on Halloween

    c. get rid of bad feelings

7. Where does the custom of a wedding veil come from?

    a. Turkey

    b. Greece

    c. Iran

8. What does the Chinese custom of <u>feng shui</u> relate to?

    a. placing objects in a home

    b. dressing correctly for weddings

    c. being successful in school

Before You Read

A. Work in groups. Describe a traditional wedding ceremony in your culture. Use the questions below to help you.

1. Which month is most popular for weddings?
2. What time of the day is common for weddings?
3. What day of the week is common for weddings?
4. What kind of ceremony do you have?
5. Who is in the wedding party?
6. What kind of clothes do the people in the wedding party wear?
7. Where does the wedding reception take place?
8. How long does the wedding reception last?
9. What kind of food is served at the wedding reception?
10. What kind of music or dancing is there at the wedding reception?

customs
couple
~~bouquet~~
aunt
stamp
~~veil~~
sister
bride
Roman
envelope
rituals
Chinese

B. Work with a partner. Write two words from the list that are related to each numbered word.

1. garter   <u> bouquet </u>   <u>   veil   </u>

2. invitation   <u>   </u>   <u>   </u>

3. grandmother   <u>   </u>   <u>   </u>

4. fiance   <u>   </u>   <u>   </u>

5. traditions   <u>   </u>   <u>   </u>

6. Greek   <u>   </u>   <u>   </u>

A Lucky Time to Get Married

Karen Christiansen in Madison, Wisconsin, is licking stamps and addressing envelopes. Soon she and her fiance will be sending out invitations to their June wedding. Meanwhile, on the other side of the world, Wei Yashung is at the hairdresser in Shanghai, China. She knows she will have a long wait—maybe four hours. It's May 18, the most popular day to get married in China. The room is filled with brides preparing for their special day.

Weddings are a special event in every culture. People begin new lives together and families are joined.

"Everyone feels very emotional at this time. There are a lot of rituals and superstitions at weddings," says Maxine Rowe, an anthropologist who studies weddings.

As Karen plans her wedding, her aunt and her sisters help her check off the things she needs according to an old custom. They recite the traditional verse, "Something old, something new, something borrowed, and something blue." Female friends and relatives gather around and contribute grandmother's locket, a cousin's wedding veil, or a blue garter to prepare the bride for the ceremony.

Many wedding traditions in western cultures began long ago and were designed to protect the couple from bad luck. "The wedding veil is a Greek custom intended to hide the bride from evil spirits," says Maxine. "The Romans contributed the custom of bridesmaids—women dressed like the bride—to confuse the spirits. Wedding bouquets had strong-smelling herbs like rosemary, thyme, and garlic to scare away witches and devils."

In China, Yashung and her fiance are one of thousands of couples that have chosen May 18 for their wedding day. "In the past, Chinese couples consulted an almanac to find lucky and unlucky days for getting married," explains Maxine. "But in modern times a new tradition is being formed." The eighteenth day of the fifth month, five-one-eight or "wu yao ba" as it is called in China, sounds very close to "wo yao fa," or "I will get rich." It is considered a good omen to get married on this day.

So in Shanghai, Yashung waits with the other young women. She is trying on a glittering silver dress that she is planning to wear later at the wedding banquet. "Why am I getting married today?" she repeats when asked the question. "Everybody knows why. It's May 18! That means I will get rich!"

Some people don't think it's a good idea for everyone to get married on the same day. "It's silly and superstitious," a newspaper reporter wrote. But hairdressers, florists, and owners of restaurants and limousine services say it's the best day of the year. They can raise their prices for this one day and their services are fully booked. Maybe they are the ones who should be saying, "I will get rich."

Reading Skills

READING COMPREHENSION

Read the questions and write the answers.

1. What is in the envelopes that Karen is addressing?

    wedding invitations

2. Why will Yashung have a long wait at the hairdresser?

_____

3. Why do people feel so emotional about weddings?

_____

4. Who is Maxine Rowe? _____

5. What parts of the traditional verse do "grandmother's locket"

and "a blue garter" represent? _____ and

_____

6. What part of the verse does the wedding veil represent?

_____

7. What was the original purpose of bridesmaids?

_____

8. How could wedding bouquets protect the bride from evil

spirits?

_____

_____

9. In China the pronunciation of "I will get rich" sounds like

which date?

_____

10. Who really gets rich on May 18 in Shanghai?

_____

_____

SKIM TO CHECK THE INFORMATION

Read the sentences and write T *for* true *or* F *for* false *according to information in the story. Correct the false information.*

1. June is a popular month to get married in China. ___F__in___

   _____North America_____

2. In China, people often get married in the summer or fall. _____

3. Weddings are special events everywhere in the world. _____

4. People feel very emotional at the time of a wedding. _____

5. There are a lot of rituals at weddings. _____

6. Many western brides wear something old at their weddings.

   _____

7. Many western wedding traditions are quite new. _____

8. Modern brides often carry strong-smelling herbs in their bouquets. _____

9. Choosing May 18 for a wedding in China is an ancient tradition. _____

10. The sounds for May 18 are similar to "I will be happy." _____

11. Everyone agrees that May 18 is a good day to get married in China. _____

12. Hairdressers and florists in China make more money on May 18 than on any other day. _____

BUILD YOUR VOCABULARY

Match the words to the definitions.

1. a sign of what will happen __g__

2. a big fancy car ____

3. a kind of necklace ____

4. a reference book ____

5. a person engaged to be married ____

6. a veil ____

7. kinds of herbs ____

8. a person who studies cultures ____

9. a bunch of flowers ____

10. things used to send invitations ____

a. a bouquet
b. stamps and envelopes
c. an anthropologist
d. a locket
e. rosemary and thyme
f. an almanac
~~g~~. an omen
h. a limousine
i. something used to cover the face
j. a fiance

RECYCLE THE VOCABULARY

In each group of four words, cross out the word that doesn't match.

1. restaurant	hairdresser	florist	~~almanac~~
2. fiance	couple	banquet	bride
3. stamps	reception	envelopes	invitations
4. prices	traditions	customs	rituals
5. bouquet	veil	locket	spirits
6. aunt	sister	bridesmaid	grandmother
7. devils	feelings	witches	evil spirits
8. prepare	plan	confuse	get ready
9. friends	relatives	bouquet	families
10. rosemary	thyme	garlic	day

CREATING HARMONY

Before You Read

A. Discuss these questions in groups.

1. Do you believe in good luck and bad luck?
2. Do you have any rituals or special objects to bring good luck?
3. What are some things people do to make their homes feel cozy and comfortable?
4. Do you know about any rituals for the house? What are they?

B. Read this paragraph. Then close your book and write it as your teacher dictates it.

In traditional cultures, people have ceremonies and rituals for driving out evil spirits and bringing good luck. People in modern cultures are not so different. Many customs that we practice today are supposed to protect us from bad luck and bring peace and harmony into our lives. What do you do for good luck?

Creating Harmony

A. Mia, a woman with long dark hair, stands in the middle of an apartment and chants a song. Then she lights a dried herb called sage, which she calls a "smudge." The strong smell is supposed to drive away bad spirits. Mia is cleansing the apartment for Lisa and Edouardo, a young couple who are getting married.

B. When Lisa and Edouardo decided to marry, they went looking for a new apartment. They wanted to start their lives together in a fresh setting. The problem was that rents were high and Lisa's apartment was very reasonable. They wouldn't find as good a deal anywhere else. So they called in a smudger.

C. "I decided to have the apartment smudged," says Lisa. "That means getting out all the bad stuff, the bad spirits. I'm kind of spiritual, so I wanted to get a clean start. That's why I called Mia, a smudger." Mia describes herself as a spiritualist, a person who drives bad spirits away. "I can get rid of the spirits of old boyfriends or girlfriends, husbands or wives. Anyone you want to get rid of—I can make their spirits leave," she says.

D. Smudging is an ancient American Indian ritual for driving out bad spirits. The tradition lives on in many lands. Smudgers use bluing, a laundry liquid, around door frames in Mexico and the southwestern United States. The ancient Greeks had a similar ritual. "My family used to do this in Colombia too," says Ricardo Lopez, who writes about different cultures. "The neighbors would come over and burn different kinds of herbs to get rid of evil spirits. I don't know if it really worked, but people seemed to feel better afterwards."

E. Some people compare smudging to the Chinese art of feng shui, which is becoming increasingly well known in western cultures. Feng shui is an ancient folk art that tells you how to set up your home. According to the theories, moving objects and furniture or changing the colors in a room can help balance the energy in a house. The correct placement of objects can bring harmony and good luck.

F. One woman describes the changes she made to her home

after a feng shui consultation. "I painted the living room light green to bring good fortune and put in lots of plants. I put plants in the entrance to every room and I put a mirror near the door to my office. I don't know if it works, but I feel very cozy and satisfied with my house."

G. Lisa and Edouardo are happy with their cleansed apartment, too. The ritual began when Mia arrived with oils, crystals, and semi-precious stones. She played soft music and lit the herbs. She laid out the crystals to absorb negativity and put out beads to symbolize fertility and a happy home life. When she left, Lisa and Edouardo returned to their apartment. "The apartment feels much better now. We seem to be getting along better—more in harmony with each other. It feels different," Lisa says.

Reading Skills

READ FOR THE MAIN IDEA

Circle the letter of the main idea of this story.

a. Mia's ceremony

b. using crystals and oils to chase away bad spirits

c. how people try to create a harmonious home

d. American Indian customs

READING COMPREHENSION

Find <u>four</u> correct ways to complete each sentence according to information from the story.

1. Smudging is

   ✓ a way to drive away bad spirits.

   ____ an American Indian ritual.

   ____ a way to clean a dirty apartment.

_____ similar to a Greek ritual.

_____ a way to gct rid of negativity.

_____ a tradition that began in China.

_____ a way to get rid of bad smells.

2. Some rituals used in smudging include

_____ lighting a strong-smelling herb.

_____ standing outside the door of the apartment.

_____ getting rid of old boyfriends or girlfriends.

_____ putting out oils and crystals.

_____ chanting a song.

_____ using a laundry liquid called bluing.

_____ playing music on the radio.

3. Feng shui is

_____ an ancient folk art.

_____ a way to prepare food.

_____ concerned with the correct placement of objects.

_____ used in Colombia.

_____ used more in apartments than in houses.

_____ designed to bring harmony and good luck.

_____ becoming well known in western cultures.

4. Some rituals used in feng shui include

_____ painting rooms certain colors.

_____ putting mirrors near doors.

_____ burning strong-smelling herbs.

_____ putting plants in entrance ways.

_____ using laundry liquid to wash the walls.

_____ using beads to symbolize fertility.

_____ the correct placement of objects.

5. After using smudging or feng shui, people reported

_____ feeling more in harmony with others.

_____ getting along better with others.

_____ feeling nervous and depressed.

_____ feeling like they got a bad deal.

_____ feeling cozy and satisfied.

_____ feeling the same.

_____ feeling different.

USE THE CONTEXT TO FIND THE MEANING

Locate the numbered words below in the story and use the context to understand how each one is used. Then circle the letter of the word or phrase that means the same thing.

1. cleansing (paragraph A)

   a. washing the house   (b.) renewing the atmosphere in a house

2. setting (paragraph B)

   a. time   b. environment

3. reasonable (paragraph B)

   a. inexpensive   b. well-located

4. stuff (paragraph C)

   a. feelings   b. smells

5. get rid of (paragraph C)

   a. attract   b. remove

6. ancient (paragraph D)

    a. difficult   b. old

7. ritual (paragraph D)

    a. ceremony   b. trick

8. cozy (paragraph F)

    a. proud   b. comfortable

9. negativity (paragraph G)

    a. odors   b. bad feelings

10. to be getting along (paragraph G)

    a. to be relating to   b. to be leaving
       someone

RECYCLE THE VOCABULARY

Match the List A items to the List B items.

List A

1. get rid of ___i___

2. play ____

3. balance ____

4. move ____

5. paint ____

6. change the ____

7. write about ____

8. get a clean ____

9. feel ____

10. look for an ____

11. decide to ____

12. start their lives ____

List B

a. soft music

b. objects and furniture

c. the living room

d. color

e. different cultures

f. start

g. together

h. apartment

~~i.~~ bad spirits

j. the energy

k. marry

l. cozy and satisfied

Put It Together

A. Match the words in List A with the examples in List B.

List A

1. beliefs __d__

2. objects used in rituals ____

3. relationships ____

4. wedding objects ____

5. herbs ____

6. protection from spirits

____

7. businesses ____

8. spirits ____

List B

a. couple, fiance, wife, girlfriend

b. restaurants, limousines, hair-dressers

c. oils, crystals, semiprecious stones

~~d.~~ rituals, traditions, customs

e. herbs, veil, bridesmaids

f. witches, devils

g. garter, bouquet, locket, veil

h. sage, rosemary, thyme, garlic

B. Classify the words by completing the chart.

	Belief or Tradition	Action	Feeling	Object	Place
1. smudging	✓				
2. cleansing		✓			
3. hairdresser's shop					
4. spiritual					
5. dried sage					
6. feng shui					
7. semiprecious stones					
8. addressing envelopes					
9. veil					
10. crystals					
11. Mexico					
12. burning					
13. spiritualism					
14. cozy					
15. chanting					
16. getting married					
17. bouquet					
18. apartment					
19. rosemary					
20. harmony					

TALK ABOUT IT

Discuss these questions in groups.

1. Do you have any rituals you use for bringing good luck? What are they?

2. Do you know anyone who is very superstitious? How does this person act?

3. What are some rituals and superstitions in your culture?

TELL THE STORIES

A. Tell the story "A Lucky Time to Get Married" in pairs. One person is getting married in America. The other person is getting married in China. Describe how you prepare for your wedding and what takes place at the wedding. Use the information from the story and add your own information.

B. Tell the story "Creating Harmony." Imagine you want to cleanse your apartment or home in order to make a fresh start. Describe why you hired a smudger or a feng shui consultant. Explain what the person does and how you feel afterwards.

WRITING OPTION

A. Write about a traditional celebration in your culture.

B. Write about a wedding. You can write about your own wedding or the wedding of a friend or family member. Describe what happened in as much detail as you can.

BEYOND THE STORIES

A. Look in the newspaper for a story about a custom or ritual. Bring the article to class. Talk about the custom and when and how it takes place.

B. Do a survey about getting married. Ask three people outside of class about marriage customs or rituals in their culture. Share your information in the next class. What similarities are there between cultures? What unique information did you get?

UNIT 6

Heroes

STORY 1   NEVER STOP MOVING

STORY 2   SEARCH-AND-RESCUE MOM

Let's Get Ready

A. What does it mean to be a hero? Work in groups. Think of some heroes. Discuss what makes these people heroes.

B. Look at the list of words below. Which ones apply to the heroes you thought of?

brave

intelligent

skilled

a risk taker

generous

courageous

strong

persistent

serious

energetic

NEVER STOP MOVING

Before You Read

This story is about the father of modern jazz dancing. Work with a partner. Look at the lists of words below.

1. talented dancer, singer, contest winner
2. car crash, coma, unconscious, paralyzed
3. hospital, dance class, falling, trying
4. Hollywood, movies, teacher, famous

A. Discuss what you think happens in the story, and give a rough outline of the story.

B. Write questions about information you would like to have.

Never Stop Moving

A. Luigi Facciuto is considered the father of modern jazz dancing. He teaches his famous dance technique, called "Luigi Style," to Broadway and Hollywood stars in his New York studio. But years ago, after a terrible car crash, he was told he would never walk again.
B. Luigi was born on March 20, 1925, in Stubenville, Ohio, to a family of five boys and three girls. His parents were Italian immigrants who met in Ohio. As a child, Luigi was a talented dancer and singer. At the age of five, he began to enter amateur contests, singing,

tap dancing, and doing acrobatics. He always won first prize. When he was nine years old, a talent scout saw him and Luigi got his first professional job. He quickly became known as a talented singer and dancer and was able to make a good living as a performer.
C. Then one day his world changed. On a rainy December day in Los Angeles, Luigi set out to buy ballet shoes. The driver of the car he was riding in lost control, and the car skidded on the wet Hollywood street. Luigi was thrown out of the car. His head was crushed against a curb and he was almost killed. He was in a coma for twenty-two days, then unconscious for a month. The accident left the right side of his body and the left side of his face paralyzed. His jaw and teeth were broken, and his eyes were completely crossed. When he woke up, the doctors told him, "You'll never walk again. You're paralyzed."
D. "As I lay in bed, a voice in my head kept saying, 'Don't stop moving, kid. If you stop moving then you are dead. Never stop moving,'" says Luigi. "I knew I couldn't just lie there for the rest of my life.

I loved to dance, and I wasn't going to give up."

E. When he left the hospital two months later, Luigi still couldn't stand without support. But he was determined to learn to dance again, and he returned to dance school. His brother-in-law Frank supported his weight as Luigi took dance classes and practiced hard until he was finally able to walk on his own. Some days his teacher left the dance class crying, begging Frank to take Luigi out of the dance classes because he kept falling and bleeding.

F. Luigi persisted. "I learned where the muscles begin and end. I wasn't concentrating on any one muscle. I was learning to control my whole body," he says. "I didn't want people to look at my injured face, I wanted them to see my body, so I tried to make it look beautiful."

G. Luigi was so successful in regaining control of his body that a talent scout approached him about dancing in a movie. Luigi didn't get that part, but he soon got other parts. He became well known as a dancer and began to get jobs without even having to audition. For eight years, he worked as a chorus dancer in major Hollywood films. No one realized that he was still partially paralyzed. He always found ways to tilt his head back slightly so people would look at his body instead of his face.

H. While working on movies, Luigi developed a personalized technique to warm up his muscles and help him stay flexible. On the movie sets, he would practice his routine so he wouldn't fall down during the filming. Other dancers noticed his technique and began to copy him. Sometimes ten or twenty dancers at a time were following his routine, saying, "Please teach us, Luigi. It's so beautiful." After a while, he began to teach classes in his special "classical jazz" style. He soon attracted famous dancers, actors, and athletes from around the world who came to learn his unique style. Many of the top names in musical theater, dance, and film came to study with him.

I. To celebrate his 65th birthday, the City of New York named Wednesday, March 21, 1990, "Luigi Day." Hundreds of friends and associates came to honor the international performer and beloved dance teacher who had influenced them for over forty years. Luigi simply said, "In order to be a great dancer, you have to be a human being first."

Reading Skills

Answer the questions with exact information from the story. Use the number of words suggested.

1. Luigi was told he would never walk again (5 words)

   _____*after a terrible car crash*_____.

2. Luigi was nine when he got his first (2 words)

   _____.

3. The car skidded when the driver of the car (2 words)

   _____.

4. Doctors said Luigi would (3 words) _____.

5. The message of the voice in Luigi's head said, "Never (2 words)

   _____."

6. When Luigi left the hospital, he couldn't (1 word/1 word)

   _____ without _____.

7. Frank was Luigi's (1 word) _____.

8. Luigi was learning to control his (2 words) _____.

9. When Luigi became famous, he didn't have to (1 word)

   _____ for parts.

10. Although he worked in many Hollywood films, people didn't

    realize that Luigi was still (2 words) _____.

11. Luigi practiced his routine on the set so he wouldn't (5 words)

    _____.

12. Famous people he taught included (3 words)

    _____, _____, and _____.

VOCABULARY IN CONTEXT

Scan the story. Find words that mean the opposite of the words below.

1. Paragraph A: studies _____teaches_____

                     wonderful _____

2. Paragraph B: professional _____

                     never _____

3. Paragraph C: sunny _____

                     conscious _____

4. Paragraph D: alive _____

                     hated _____

5. Paragraph E: entered _____

                     laughing _____

6. Paragraph F: gave up _____

                     ugly _____

7. Paragraph G: minor _____

                     completely _____

8. Paragraph H: rigid _____

                     unknown _____

9. Paragraph I: enemies _____

                     last _____

UNDERSTAND FACT AND OPINION

A fact is something you can see or prove. An opinion is what someone thinks or believes. Read these sentences with a partner. Decide if the information is a fact or an opinion. Write F for fact or O for opinion.

1. Luigi teaches his dance technique to Broadway and Hollywood stars. __F__

2. Luigi got his first professional job when he was nine years old. _____

3. Luigi was in an accident because the driver of the car was driving carelessly. _____

4. If Luigi ever stopped moving, he would die. _____

5. Luigi fought hard to recover because he was a proud man. _____

6. Luigi was in the hospital for four months. _____

7. If Frank hadn't helped him, Luigi wouldn't have been able to walk again. _____

8. Some days, the teacher left the dance class crying. _____

9. Luigi's technique to warm up his muscles was better than any other technique. _____

10. In order to be a great dancer, you have to be a human being first. _____

Before You Read

A. Discuss these questions in groups.

1. What does "search and rescue" mean?

2. What are some natural disasters where people need to be rescued?

3. What are some ways to find people who are lost?

4. Which animals can help locate missing people?

B. Read this paragraph. Then close your book and write it as your teacher dictates it.

The average dog can smell 200 times better than the average human can. Dogs can smell things that people can't smell at all. Dogs are used to look for lost children. They can also locate people who are buried by earthquakes or other disasters. Maybe this is one reason that a dog is called man's best friend.

Search-and-Rescue Mom

A. When Caroline Hebard heard the phone ring late in the evening, she knew it was something important. She listened as a park ranger explained the situation. Seven children were lost in the Pennsylvania wilderness. Caroline pulled on her red jacket that said RESCUE on it and called to her dog, Aly, a German shepherd. She and Aly raced to their rescue truck and climbed in. Then Caroline put on the emergency light and stepped on the gas. She knew they had no time to lose. Caroline's own four children waved good-bye.

B. In the dark Pennsylvania woods, Caroline and Aly walked for hours looking for signs of the children. It was a freezing autumn night, and Caroline soon became cold and exhausted. Suddenly she saw footprints ahead. In the cold, it was difficult for Aly to pick up the children's scent, but finally he found it and began to bark. Soon they saw more footprints. Then two miles down the road, Aly began to yelp with joy and Caroline began to run. There were the children. They were shivering and crying, but they were safe!

C. Caroline Hebard is a pioneer in canine search and rescue, and she and Aly are a specialized team with many amazing, life-saving rescues to their credit. It's an unusual career for a mother of four. Caroline studied languages in college and planned to teach, but she wanted a physical challenge in her work. She had always loved dogs and used to raise them as a hobby. One day a friend suggested canine search-and-rescue work. "I loved the suggestion," says Caroline. "I always wanted to work with dogs, so this seemed like a natural choice."

D. Caroline and Aly make an excellent team. Dogs have a great sensitivity to smell. "They can sniff out things a human could never locate," says Caroline. She trained Aly to find the scent of humans underground and in open spaces. Caroline is a natural athlete who skis and mountain climbs, and she is highly skilled in wilderness survival. She and Aly can find people faster than a dozen human searchers can. Caroline also speaks seven languages, so she often translates for other rescue workers when she works in different countries.

E. Caroline and Aly travel all over the world for their work. After the terrible earthquake in Mexico City, many people were trapped in the collapsed buildings. Caroline knew how dangerous it was to go inside, but she and Aly crawled through building after building searching for survivors anyway. Aly found a woman who had been trapped for a week without food or water. She was too weak to call for help. Caroline helped rescue 22 people in 68 separate buildings. She also remembers earthquakes in Japan and El Salvador. She'll never forget people's desperate cries of, "Find my wife!" "Find my husband!" "Find my child!" "Help me, please!"

F. Each time Caroline returns home from one of her missions, her children greet her with words of encouragement—"Great work, Mom! Way to go!" Then Caroline turns her attention to family matters, such as her children's soccer practices and school dances. But the memories of the suffering she has seen stay with her for a long time.

G. People ask Caroline why she is willing to risk her life like this. The work is physically and emotionally demanding and the pay is minimal. "The rewards come from helping people in distress," she says simply. "Someone has to do this work."

Reading Skills

SKIM FOR THE MAIN IDEAS

Skim the text and find the paragraph that tells about each of the following topics:

1. Caroline and Aly's work in other countries __E__

2. rescuing lost children in Pennsylvania ____

3. Caroline and Aly's abilities for rescue work ____

4. how Caroline went into rescue work ____

5. setting out on a mission ____

6. why Caroline continues her rescue work ____

7. returning home ____

READING COMPREHENSION

Find three correct ways to complete each sentence according to information in the story.

1. When she gets a call for a rescue mission, Caroline

   ✓ puts on her red jacket.

   ____ does her exercises.

   ____ calls her dog, Aly.

   ____ takes her time.

   ____ says good-bye to her children.

   ____ calls her friend on the phone.

2. The search for the seven children was difficult because

   ____ Caroline became exhausted.

   ____ Caroline got lost.

   ____ it was dark.

   ____ Aly couldn't find the scent in the cold.

   ____ the children weren't crying very loudly.

   ____ other people found the children first.

3. Caroline is especially suited to search-and-rescue work because

_____ she is a mother of four.

_____ she is a natural athlete.

_____ she likes to help people.

_____ she likes physical challenges.

_____ she thinks of search-and-rescue work as a hobby.

_____ she always wanted to be a teacher.

4. Caroline and Aly are able to help people all over the world because

_____ they make a great team.

_____ Caroline can translate for other rescue workers.

_____ Caroline likes to see new places.

_____ Caroline is trained as a nurse.

_____ Caroline and Aly can find people faster than human searchers.

_____ Caroline has a good sense of direction.

RECYCLE THE VOCABULARY

In each group of four words, cross out the word that doesn't match.

1. sniff   scent   smell   ~~exhausted~~

2. German shepherd   human   dog   canine

3. child   nurse   wife   husband

4. cold   freezing   lost   shivering

5. hobby   career   job   occupation

6. situation   help   rescue   save

Put It Together

The word because *shows the cause of an action or a situation.*
Match the effects in List A with the causes in List B.

List A

1. Luigi wanted to make his body beautiful __j__

2. Caroline risks her life ____

3. Luigi returned to dance school ____

4. It was difficult for Aly to pick up the children's scent ____

5. Caroline can translate for other rescue workers ____

6. Luigi always won the first prize in contests ____

7. Caroline put on her red jacket ____

8. Other dancers wanted to learn Luigi's technique ____

9. Friends and associates honored Luigi ____

10. Luigi got jobs without having to audition ____

List B

a. because she speaks seven languages.

b. because he was their beloved dance teacher.

c. because it was so beautiful.

d. because he was very talented.

e. because he was determined to learn to dance again.

f. because she wants to help people in distress.

g. because she was on a rescue mission.

h. because the weather was very cold.

i. because he was a well-known dancer.

j. because he didn't want people to look at his injured face.

TALK ABOUT IT

Discuss these questions in groups.

1. What traits make Luigi and Caroline heroes?
2. What were the biggest challenges Luigi and Caroline had to overcome?
3. Can you think of any other people with stories similar to these?
4. If you could meet Luigi or Caroline, what would you say to them?
5. Why are some people willing to do things that others are afraid to do?
6. What traits do Luigi and Caroline have in common?

TELL THE STORIES

A. Tell the story "Never Stop Moving" to someone outside the class. Imagine you are a student in Luigi's dance class. Explain what happened to Luigi and how he began to dance again.

B. Tell the story "Search-and-Rescue Mom" to someone outside the class. Imagine you are one of the people Caroline and Aly saved after an earthquake. Explain what happened to you and how Caroline and Aly saved you.

WRITING OPTION

A. Who is your hero? Write about this person. Explain what he or she did and why you consider this person a hero.

B. Write a letter to Caroline Hebard thanking her for saving your friend after an earthquake.

BEYOND THE STORIES

A. Do a survey. Ask two people outside the class if they have a hero. Ask why they consider this person a hero. Share your ideas in the next class.

B. Look in the newspaper for stories about people who overcame hardships or performed heroic acts. Bring the stories to class and discuss them.

UNIT 7

Technoworld

STORY 1   THE WORLD IS GETTING SMALLER

STORY 2   THE MACHINE THAT KNOWS YOUR FACE

Let's Get Ready

A. Work in groups. Talk about the developments in technology that make the statements below seem funny today. Explain why.

1. In 1899, the U.S. Commissioner of Patents said, "Everything that can be invented has been invented."

2. In 1903, the president of the Michigan Savings Bank said, "The horse is here to stay, but the automobile is only a fad."

3. In 1936, a Canadian radio broadcaster said, "Television won't matter in your lifetime or mine."

4. In 1943, the chairman of IBM said, "I think there is a world market for maybe five computers."

5. In 1949, *Popular Mechanics* magazine said, "Computers in the future may weigh only 1.5 tons."

6. In 1977, the president of Digital Equipment Corporation said, "There is no reason for any individual to have a computer in his home."

B. Work in groups. In what year were your parents born? Discuss which technologies that are common today didn't exist then.

1. satellites
2. photocopying
3. cell phones
4. computers
5. Walkmans
6. washing machines
7. tape recorders
8. heart bypass surgery
9. microwave ovens
10. VCRs
11. ATMs
12. PINs
13. Polaroid cameras
14. faxes
15. E-mail
16. laptop computers
17. jet travel
18. virtual airline tickets
19. compact discs
20. cards as hotel keys

Before You Read

globe	*For each word, find two other words with related meanings.*
~~device~~	1. machine *device* *robot*
~~robot~~	2. tiny
industry	3. planet
minute	4. medicine
world	5. manufacturing
operation	6. bloodstream
heart	
factories	
injection	
microscopic	
arteries	

The World Is Getting Smaller

A. Imagine this: a television screen the size and thickness of a piece of paper. You carry it around in your pocket and take it out when you want to watch a show. Image a guitar so tiny you can't see it with the human eye, but you can hear sounds when its strings are plucked. Some people say the future is big, but when it comes to technology, the world is getting smaller.

B. Nanotechnology is the science that deals with doing things in a very small way, and it is being explored and developed all over the globe. Micromachines too small to be seen by the human eye are being designed to do many things that larger machines do today. And these machines, no larger in diameter than a human hair, are extremely powerful. Many scientists say nanotechnology will produce the next industrial revolution.

C. How small are these machines, exactly? *Nano* comes from the Greek word for *dwarf*. A nanometer is 1 one-billionth of a meter. The period at the end of this sentence can contain about 100 micrometers, which is equal to 100,000 nanometers. To understand this new technology, we

have to get rid of our normal ideas of size and strength.

D. Minute robots, called "nanobots," are being developed that will revolutionize manufacturing. Instead of cars being produced on assembly lines, for example, scientists predict that cars can be built in a giant container into which raw materials and microscopic machines have been placed. Thousands of nanobots will direct the process and tell the microscopic machines what to do.

E. Micromachines can also be used to make our environment safer. Today, poisonous chemicals are stored in containers or transported by trucks or trains. This sometimes results in dangerous spills. But with nanotechnology, manufacturers could have their own tiny chemical factories. These factories would be no bigger than a sugar cube and would manufacture exactly the amount of chemicals needed at the moment. No chemicals would need to be stored or transported. The workplace would be safer, and the environment would be cleaner.

F. Maybe the area where nanotechnology will have the biggest impact is medical science. Imagine

nanobots in medicine. Thousands or even millions of tiny machines can be sent into the human body with specific missions. For example, they can be designed to find and destroy cancer cells or viruses. Other machines may stay in the human body permanently to help organs that are not functioning properly.
G. Think of the possibilities in using such tiny machines in surgery. Imagine machines so small you can swallow them in a capsule or inject them into your bloodstream through a needle. After you've had too many years of junk food, these tiny robots could be sent into your arteries to clean them. An intelligent machine in your heart would look around to find the problem and then repair it. If you needed an operation, it would be almost like swallowing the surgeon.
H. When could all of this happen? Scientists predict that much of this is possible in the next 30 years. After all, when your grandparents were young, they would have laughed if someone told them a person could walk on the moon. Thousands of scientists around the world are working on these micromachines. Nanotechnology is just around the corner.

Reading Skills

SKIM FOR THE MAIN IDEAS

A. Skim the story. Find the paragraph that tells about each of the following topics. Paragraph A is the introduction; omit that paragraph.

1. how small nanomachines are __C__

2. new developments in manufacturing ____

3. a definition of nanotechnology ____

4. general uses in medicine ____

5. when to expect nanotechnology to be used ____

6. nanobots and the environment ____

7. uses in surgery ____

B. Circle the words in the first sentence of each paragraph that helped you know what kind of information the paragraph contained. Omit paragraph A.

UNDERSTAND CAUSE AND EFFECT

The words because, so, that, in order to, **and** since **show the cause of an action or a situation. Match the causes in List A with the effects in List B.**

List A

1. Nanotechnology is so powerful that ___g___

2. A TV screen is like a piece of paper so _____

3. We have to change our ideas of size and strength in order to

   _____

4. Tiny machines will be sent into the human body in order to

   _____

5. Minidevices may stay in the human body in order to _____

6. Chemicals could be manufactured as needed, so _____

7. You have eaten too much junk food, so _____

8. Medical instruments will be so tiny that _____

List B

a. you can swallow them in a capsule.

b. help organs that aren't functioning.

c. find and destroy cancer cells.

d. your arteries could be blocked.

e. you can carry it in your pocket.

f. no chemicals would have to be stored or transported.

g. scientists say it will produce the next industrial revolution.

h. understand this new technology.

Find these expressions in the story. Then use the context to help you choose the expression that has the same meaning.

1. <u>in diameter</u> refers to (paragraph B)

   a. length.

   (b.) thickness.

2. <u>Nano</u> describes (paragraph C)

   a. strength.

   b. size.

3. To <u>get rid of</u> means (paragraph C)

   a. to get something new.

   b. to throw something away.

4. <u>Minute</u> means (paragraph D)

   a. tiny.

   b. big.

5. <u>Nanobots</u> are (paragraph D)

   a. big robots.

   b. small robots.

6. An <u>assembly line</u> is used to (paragraph D)

   a. manufacture products.

   b. sell products.

7. <u>Microscopic</u> means (paragraph D)

   a. very small.

   b. very big.

8. To <u>store</u> something means to (paragraph E)

   a. keep something.

   b. sell something.

9. To <u>have a big impact</u> means to (paragraph F)

   a. make a difference.

   b. stay the same.

10. <u>A mission</u> is (paragraph F)

   a. something you intend to do.

   b. something you don't want to do.

11. To <u>swallow</u> means (paragraph G)

   a. to inject.

   b. to eat.

12. <u>Just around the corner</u> means (paragraph H)

   a. later.

   b. soon.

THE MACHINE THAT KNOWS YOUR FACE

Before You Read

A. Discuss these questions in groups.

1. What is a PIN?
2. What are some places that use PINs?
3. How many PINs do you have?
4. What happens if you forget your PIN?
5. What other security devices do you know about?

B. Match the words in List A to the words in List B.

List A

1. a part of the eye ___f___

2. something that knows your voice

   _____

3. what you go through when you

   travel to another country _____

4. part of your finger _____

5. a code _____

6. another word for machine _____

List B

a. a password or a PIN

b. device

c. voice recognition

d. border crossing

e. fingerprint

f. iris

The Machine That Knows Your Face

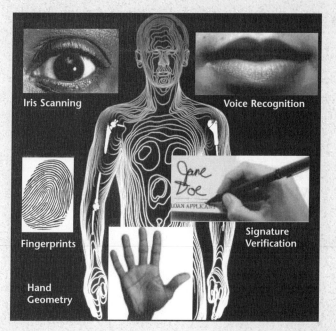

Iris Scanning

Voice Recognition

Fingerprints

Signature Verification

Hand Geometry

A. At a gas station, a man stops to cash his paycheck. A machine knows his face, and in a minute the man leaves with his cash. At a large university, students use a hand-scanning machine to get into the cafeteria. These people are using "smart machines," which can identify people by their body characteristics. These new devices use fingers, hands, faces, eyes, and voices. Some machines may even use smells. This new technology, called biometrics, gets information from parts of the body.

B. In the past, biometric machines were used mainly in government agencies or in prisons. But now the costs are lower, and these machines are starting to be used everywhere, from border crossings to daycare centers.

C. Some people are concerned about privacy. They worry that the machines will get personal information about them. "Actually, biometric machines help protect our privacy," says Jay Tarkett, who works at a company that develops the machines. "They can be used instead of passwords on a computer, for example. They can also identify criminals or terrorists at airports, so they help promote public safety."

D. Some people don't like the idea of using fingerprints because they associate them with criminals. And they don't work for some people, such as bricklayers, who wear down their fingerprints. But face recognition works well because the subject doesn't have to do anything. To cash a check at a bank, the customer would look at a machine similar to an automatic teller. If the face matches the picture kept on file, the customer gets the money with no problem.

E. The hand scan works well in the college cafeteria. Before the machine was used, students at the college entered the cafeteria using cards similar to credit cards. The problem was that students often lost or forgot their cards. With the hand-scanning machine, the problem was solved. "The machine works really well," says Manuela Lopez, a food services coordinator. "Students never forget their hands when they come to the cafeteria!"

F. But the machines are still new, and there can be problems. For example, voice recognition works on the phone, but it is not precise and can be tricked. Machines that use face recognition can be fooled if people dye their hair or gain a lot of weight. This particular problem may be solved by a new type of technology that scans the iris, the colored part of a person's eyes. It can even identify the person from a few feet away, so it may be able to recognize a customer as he or she approaches the ATM.

G. The hand scan at the university had some problems as well, at first. "At the beginning of the school year, many of the girls wore their boyfriend's rings. If they stopped wearing the rings later, the machine rejected them," says Manuela. "Now we have a newer machine, and it can cope with the missing ring problem."

H. "Some people don't want to use machines that take their pictures," says Jay Tarkett. "But other people are happy to use the biometric machines. You don't have to carry a bank card or remember your PIN (personal identification number). And if you lose your check, no one can cash it."

Reading Skills

Read the questions and write the answers on the lines.

1. What is biometrics?

    a new technology that gets information from parts of the body

2. Why are biometric machines starting to be used more widely?

    _____

3. Why do some people worry about privacy?

    _____

4. How can biometrics promote public safety?

    _____

5. Why do some people not like the idea of using fingerprints?

    _____

6. What is the biggest advantage of face-recognition technology?

    _____

7. What was the problem at the cafeteria before the hand-scanning machine?

    _____

8. Why does the system work well now, according to Manuela?

    _____

9. What is the problem with voice-recognition technology?

    _____

10. How can face-recognition machines be fooled?

    _____

11. How can this problem be solved?

_____

12. What are some things people don't need when they use biometric machines?

_____

USE THE CONTEXT TO FIND THE MEANING

Locate the underlined words below in the story and use the context to understand how the words are used. Then write the words or ideas that the underlined words refer to.

1. Paragraph A: These people are using . . . ___a man, students___

2. Paragraph B: . . . these machines are starting . . . _____

3. Paragraph C: . . . personal information about them. . . .

_____

4. Paragraph C: They can also identify . . . _____

5. Paragraph D: . . . because they associate . . . _____

6. Paragraph D: And they don't work . . . _____

7. Paragraph F: . . . but it is not precise . . . _____

8. Paragraph F: This particular problem . . . _____

9. Paragraph F: . . . it can cope with . . . _____

10. Paragraph G: . . . no one can cash it. . . . _____

ARGUMENTS FOR AND AGAINST

Look at the statements below. Some statements are in favor of using biometrics and others are against. Complete the chart.

	For Biometrics	Against Biometrics
1. There are concerns about privacy.		✓
2. They can be used instead of passwords.		
3. It helps promote public safety.		
4. Fingerprints are associated with criminals.		
5. Fingerprints don't work for bricklayers.		
6. Students never forget their hands.		
7. People can fake their voices on the phone.		
8. Face recognition can be fooled by dyed hair or weight gain.		
9. You don't have to carry a bank card with you.		
10. No one else can cash your checks.		

Put It Together

Use the words below to complete the crossword puzzle.

arteries
biometrics
virus
revolutionize
cafeteria
fingerprint
transport
globe
swallow
recognition
password
teller
scientists

Across

4. another word for *world*

5. something you do when you eat

7. to move something from one place to another

9. an ATM is an automatic _____ machine.

11. a code for a computer

12. the technology that uses body parts for identification

Down

1. Some machines use face _____ to identify people.

2. Some scientists say nanotechnology will _____ the world.

3. A _____ is often used to identify a criminal.

5. experts in science

6. parts of the body that carry blood

8. a kind of restaurant

10. a kind of illness

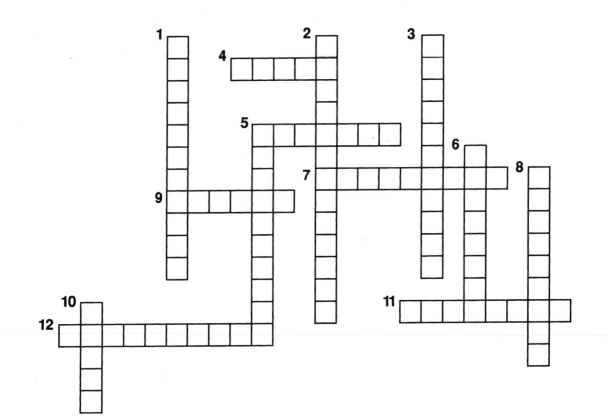

TALK ABOUT IT

Discuss these questions in groups.

1. How do you think technology will change our lives in the future?

2. How do you think people will do the following things twenty years from now:
   - send information
   - travel
   - prepare food
   - work
   - do housework

TELL THE STORIES

A. Tell the story "The World Is Getting Smaller." Explain the following:

- the meaning of *nano, nanotechnology,* and *nanobots*
- the kinds of small machines we will have in the future
- the benefits of these small machines

B. Tell the story "The Machine That Knows Your Face." Imagine that your bank begins to use the face-scanning machine. Your friend accompanies you to the bank and is surprised to see this strange new machine. Explain how the machine works and the benefits of the machine as well as the problems. Describe other types of biometric machines.

WRITING OPTION

A. Write to your bank manager to express concern about new technology the bank is using. Ask the manager to explain what the bank is using, and why.

B. Exchange letters with another student. Answer each other's letter, explaining why the new technology will benefit customers.

BEYOND THE STORIES

Do a survey. Ask three people outside the class about machines they use or know about. Ask about machines:

- in banks
- in their place of work
- at home

Compare your information in the next class. How many machines did you come up with? Make a list.

Paradise Lost

STORY 1   CAN YOU COPYRIGHT PARADISE?

STORY 2   THE LAST FRONTIER

Let's Get Ready

A. Discuss these questions in groups.

1. Did you ever want to get away to your own private paradise?
2. Where would you go?
3. How long would you stay?
4. Why would you choose this place?

B. Work in groups. Look at the list below and choose the things you would most like to have in your private paradise.

1. wide open spaces with few people
2. places to get espresso coffee
3. art galleries with Renaissance paintings
4. small villages
5. unspoiled nature
6. a beautiful landscape

7. a warm, sunny climate
8. snow-capped mountains
9. exotic animals like elk and bear
10. a feeling of adventure
11. delicious meals with local produce
12. a picturesque countryside
13. interesting places to go hiking
14. a sense of history

STORY 1   CAN YOU COPYRIGHT PARADISE?

Before You Read

Discuss these questions in groups.

1. Where is Tuscany?

2. Why is it well known?

3. Why do so many tourists like to visit this region?

4. What are some foods that come from this region?

5. Some people call Tuscany "paradise." Can you think of any reasons why?

Can You Copyright Paradise?

A. To Bill and Marge Polanski of Chicago, Illinois, Tuscany seemed like the perfect place for a vacation. The tourist brochure read, "Immerse yourselves in Italian culture in a typical Tuscan village. Walk through the vineyards and olive groves. Taste Tuscany's extraordinary cuisine. Enjoy art treasures that have survived untouched for thousands of years." The Polanskis aren't the only ones to be attracted to Tuscany's charms. They will join countless other tourists with the same idea of finding paradise on earth. But for the people of Tuscany, the charms of their region are a mixed blessing.

B. Tuscany, Italy, may be one of the best-known places in the world. Its rolling hills, small villages, and olive trees are familiar to us through Renaissance paintings and Italian novels and movies. It is in the heart of Italy and includes the cities of Florence, Sienna, and Pisa. Tuscany is considered one of the most desirable places to live in the world.

C. More than 32 million tourists visit Tuscany every year and return home to rave about its charms. Of course, advertisers and photographers are interested in the region, too. "We chose this region for its beauty," says Linda Fabris, who works for a large advertising agency. "No other place can really compare."

D. But now the scene is changing. Driving along through the countryside, you can see advertisements for Japanese cars, crackers, pantyhose, and even toilet paper. Giant orange and white pylons, over 200 feet high, dot the hills southeast of Florence. They support the 380,000-watt power lines that are strung across the hills.

E. Residents are protesting. They are afraid of losing their heritage, the region that has remained virtually untouched since the Middle Ages. Tuscans have come up with a proposal to copyright their landscape to restrict the way the countryside is used for advertising. "We are not trying to stop progress," insists Roberto Di Tommaso, a businessman. "We are simply trying to stop non-Tuscan brand names from advertising here."

F. At the same time, the promotion of Tuscany is increasing overseas.

With the opening of Tuscan Square in New York City, Tuscan products are once again in the spotlight, and the preservation of this region is more important than ever. There is even a voluntary trademark, "Made in Tuscany," to guarantee the quality of the olive oils, cheeses, and wines that come from the district. The aim is to show people that many of the products, especially foods, that use the name Tuscany, do not actually come from that region.

G. Some people say that Tuscany is so beautiful that no one can ruin it, but some residents are not so sure. "We are not saying all the advertising should be removed," Mr. Di Tommaso explains. "We just have to find a different way to do it. We have to protect the landscape that we have enjoyed for centuries. This is our cultural heritage. It should be preserved for humanity."

Reading Skills

SKIM FOR THE MAIN IDEAS

Skim the story to check the information below. Decide which paragraph focuses on each of the following ideas. Paragraph A is the introduction; omit that paragraph.

1. the ideal vacation spot __C__

2. the Tuscan landscape ____

3. ideas for preserving a cultural heritage ____

4. Tuscan Square in New York City ____

5. spoiling the Tuscan landscape ____

6. why residents of Tuscany are upset ____

READING COMPREHENSION

Circle the letter of the correct completion of each sentence according to the information from the story.

1. Tuscany is in
   a. Chicago.
   b. Italy.
   c. a small village.

2. People in Tuscany enjoy
   a. great movies.
   b. wine and olive oil.
   c. paintings by modern artists.

3. The image of Tuscany first became well known because of
   a. tourists who send postcards.
   b. Italian art and literature.
   c. advertising agencies.

4. Tuscany is located
   a. in the center of Italy.
   b. on the coast of Italy.
   c. in the north of Italy.

5. Driving through the Tuscan countryside, you can now see
   a. pantyhose and other laundry.
   b. many Japanese cars.
   c. advertisements for many products.

6. Residents want to "copyright their landscape" in order to
   a. stop progress.
   b. return the region to the Middle Ages.
   c. keep their heritage.

7. The trademark "Made in Tuscany" is used to

    a. guarantee the quality of foods from the region.

    b. increase advertising in the region.

    c. bring people to Tuscan Square.

8. Mr. Di Tommaso thinks

    a. no one can ruin the beauty of the region.

    b. all advertising should be removed.

    c. the region should be preserved for humanity.

VOCABULARY IN CONTEXT

Find words in the story that mean the following:

1. Paragraph A: unchanged   _____untouched_____

                     many   _____

2. Paragraph B: books   _____

                     attractive   _____

3. Paragraph C: visitors   _____

                     say great things   _____

4. Paragraph D: landscape   _____

                     hold up   _____

5. Paragraph E: almost   _____

                     a suggestion   _____

6. Paragraph F: across the ocean   _____

                     the objective   _____

7. Paragraph G: spoil   _____

                     for everyone   _____

RECYCLE THE VOCABULARY

Match the words from the story that go together.

oil
cars
agency
villages
paper
lines
paintings
~~hills~~
heritage
names

1. rolling _____hills_____

2. small _____

3. Renaissance _____

4. Japanese _____

5. power _____

6. brand _____

7. cultural _____

8. advertising _____

9. olive _____

10. toilet _____

Before You Read

A. Work with a partner. Read this dictionary definition of the word
frontier. *Discuss what you think this story is about.*

frontier: 1. the last edge of settled country, where the wilderness begins   2. the border of an inhabited region

B. Work with a partner. Read these statements about Alaska.
Based on what you know, write **T** *for* **true** *or* **F** *for* **false.**

1. Not many people in Alaska live in cities. __F__

2. There are more women than men in Alaska. _____

3. A resident of Anchorage has a lifestyle similar to that of a

   resident of Minneapolis. _____

4. You can now receive satellite TV in Alaska. _____

5. Alaska has fewer people per square mile than other parts of

   America. _____

6. Alaska makes up only five percent of the U.S. land mass. _____

7. You can see a lot of wildlife in Alaskan cities. _____

8. Alaska attracts young people with a sense of adventure. _____

9. Alaskan residents pay higher taxes than other Americans. _____

10. Alaska's population has grown in the last few years. _____

C. Scan the story to check your answers.

The Last Frontier

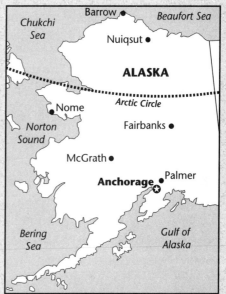

A. The image most people have of Alaska is of a remote land of ice and snow, with people living in cabins and men outnumbering women ten to one. Many people consider Alaska to be the last frontier. They see it as the last untamed piece of wilderness in America.

B. But times are changing. There are more than 600,000 residents in Alaska, and half of them live in Anchorage, a metropolitan area similar to Minneapolis or Buffalo. Most of the people live in steel-framed houses, with indoor carpets and asphalt streets.

C. Alaska is a curious mixture of old and new. Moose hunters call home on their cell phones to tell their families when they will return. People in remote villages surf the Internet and watch 28 channels of satellite TV. Drivers on the lonely stretch of highway between Anchorage and Palmer can stop for coffee at the Pit Stop Espresso Bar. There's no running water at the espresso bar however. The man who works there carries tanks of water to the restaurant every evening. Then he uses his cell phone to order the syrups to make cafe lattes as good as any in Seattle.

D. Once you pass the espresso stand, the only things you see are huge white mountains. There is still a lot of empty space. The state of Alaska makes up 16 percent of the U.S. land mass but has just one person per square mile. In the rest of the United States, the average population is 75 people per square mile. "It's different in Alaska," says Megan Sanders, a resident in a small town. "You can't get things you need easily. You have to go to Fairbanks to shop." Fairbanks is over 500 miles south of her town.

E. The wilderness can be seen even in Anchorage. Moose and elk wander into people's back yards. The streams are full of salmon. People are aware that not far from downtown is a lot of land in its natural state. The question remains—should this land be developed? The residents are divided on the question.

F. Some people see Alaska as the land of opportunity. They talk of opening shopping malls and expanding the cities. Alaska attracts young people with a sense of adventure. The population is growing, and there's a sense of spirit and economic opportunity. Alaska also attracts people who want to make money. Alaskans pay less in taxes than the residents of any other state.

G. Many people say it has already changed and will never go back. Much of the land will never be developed, but the way of life has changed. Travel is easier, and the population has grown so much that Alaska doesn't seem as remote as it once did. Perhaps it isn't a frontier after all. "I feel like we've modernized, just like anywhere else," says a resident.

Reading Skills

ARGUMENTS FOR AND AGAINST

Put these statements about Alaska into the correct category.
Complete the chart.

	Evidence of a Remote Frontier	Evidence of Typical America
1. Men outnumber women ten to one.	✓	
2. Most of the population lives in urban areas.		
3. The Anchorage-Palmer highway is lonely.		
4. People call home on their cell phones.		
5. People go into the wilds to hunt moose.		
6. You can get espresso at truck stops on the highway.		
7. There is one person per square mile.		
8. The espresso bar has no running water.		
9. People use the Internet.		
10. You may have to travel 500 miles for some supplies.		
11. Moose wander into people's back yards.		
12. Travel is easier than in the past.		
13. Some people live in cabins in the wilderness.		
14. Streets in urban centers are often made of asphalt.		

Write a paragraph to argue either that Alaska is the last frontier
or that Alaska is like any other part of the United States.

CLASSIFY THE EXAMPLES

Match the words in List A with the examples in List B.

List A

1. distance __i__

2. technology _____

3. coffee _____

4. wildlife _____

5. opportunity _____

6. landscape _____

7. house _____

8. people _____

9. city _____

10. frontier _____

List B

a. carpets, steel-framed, windows

b. residents, population, hunters

c. urban, metropolitan, downtown

d. expansion, growth, adventure

e. espresso, syrups, lattes

f. moose, salmon, elk

g. natural state, remote, undeveloped

h. satellite, Internet, cell phone

i. remote, space, travel

j. mountains, ice and snow, wilderness

VOCABULARY IN CONTEXT

Find words in the story that mean the opposite of the words
below.

1. Paragraph A: civilized   __untamed__

2. Paragraph B: remote village   _____

3. Paragraph C: close   _____

morning   _____

4. Paragraph D: tiny _____

                                  visitor _____

5. Paragraph E: in agreement _____

6. Paragraph F: decreasing _____

                                  discourages _____

7. Paragraph G: more difficult _____

Put It Together

LET'S REVIEW

Make six sentences using the words from Lists A, B, and C.

List A	List B	List C
1. ~~More than 32 million tourists~~	virtually untouched	in metropolitan areas
2. Half of Alaska's residents	a lot of space	since the Middle Ages
3. Tuscany has remained	features many products	into people's back yards
4. There is still	often wander	
5. Tuscan Square	~~visit Tuscany~~	~~every year~~
6. Moose and elk	now live	from the region
		in Alaska

1. _____ More than 32 million tourists visit Tuscany every year _____ .

2. _____ .

3. _____ .

4. _____ .

5. _____ .

6. _____ .

TALK ABOUT IT

Discuss these questions in groups.

1. Do you think the people of Tuscany are right to protest the commercial signs in their area? Why or why not?
2. What other places in the world have become very commercialized?
3. What kind of restrictions, if any, should be put on commercial activity?
4. How can people stop others from commercializing their regions?
5. Do you think the changes in Alaska are good or bad? Why?
6. Would you like to live in Alaska? Why or why not?

TELL THE STORIES

A. Tell the story "Can You Copyright Paradise?" Imagine that you live in Tuscany and are distressed to see commercial signs in the countryside. Describe to a friend why you love Tuscany and how you feel about the commercialism.

B. Tell the story "The Last Frontier." Imagine that you moved to Anchorage, Alaska, two years ago. One day your friend writes you a letter saying he or she is considering moving to Alaska. Your friend asks you what it is like and what opportunities there are. Describe your living conditions and how you feel about the land.

WRITING OPTION

Write to a travel agency. Ask about a travel destination that interests you. Explain why the place interests you. Ask about places to stay, food, prices, activities, and problems you can expect.

BEYOND THE STORIES

A. Look in the travel section of the newspaper for stories about beautiful or exciting places in the world. Bring the stories to class and present them to a small group. Discuss what makes these places exciting or interesting and why people want to go there. Then use the information to convince a partner that this is the ideal vacation spot.

B. Do a survey. Ask three people outside the class which places in the world they find most beautiful or interesting and why. Share your information in the next class. Which places were mentioned most often? Which unusual places did people suggest?

UNIT 9

How Do You Feel?

STORY 1   HAS THE CAT GOT YOUR TONGUE?

STORY 2   A PRESCRIPTION FOR MOZART

Let's Get Ready

Match the words and phrases with the examples.

1. timid character   _f_

2. professions _____

3. body organs _____

4. cures _____

5. medical problems _____

6. composers _____

7. extroverted personality _____

a. Bach, Beethoven, Chopin, Tchaikovsky, Mozart
b. lungs, heart, liver, kidneys
c. confident, well adjusted, spontaneous, outgoing
d. headaches, insomnia, hypertension, migraines
e. politician, entertainer, teacher, psychologist, scientist
f. self-conscious, ill at ease, nervous, uncomfortable, afraid
g. pills, prescriptions, therapy, herbal medicine, healing

Before You Read

A. Discuss the title. In what situations do people use this saying?

B. Work in groups. Discuss the statements and write T for true or F for false based on what you know.

1. Nearly 50 percent of North Americans are shy. __T__

2. Most shy people appear uncomfortable in social situations. ____

3. Blushing is a sign of shyness. ____

4. A shy person would be unlikely to go into politics. ____

5. Some people who appear to be snobs are actually shy. ____

6. A shy person would never become an actor or a singer. ____

7. It's possible to be born shy. ____

8. Shy parents are likely to have shy children. ____

9. Some cultures have more shy people than others. ____

10. You can't do anything about being shy. ____

C. Scan the story to check your answers.

Has the Cat Got Your Tongue?

It's a classic image—a child hiding her head in her mother's skirts when she meets a stranger, or a student blushing and stammering when the teacher asks his name. The person must be shy. You may be shy yourself. But shyness isn't that common, right? Wrong. Shyness probably affects 40 to 50 percent of all people in North America. It's just that most people are shy privately. They appear confident on the surface, and in social situations they seem well adjusted. Only 15 to 20 percent of us fit the stereotype of the shy person—someone who is visibly uncomfortable with other people.

What exactly is shyness? "It's a feeling of self-consciousness," says Rita Clark, a psychologist. Shy people feel nervous and ill at ease. They may tremble, feel their hearts pound, and have butterflies in the stomach. They worry about making a bad impression on people." Shyness doesn't necessarily show on the surface. In fact, people sometimes think that shy people are snobbish and uninterested in other people when really they are just afraid to make contact.

You may be surprised to know who is actually very shy. One well-known talk-show host, whose show is watched by millions of viewers, has to plan performances down to the last detail—in order to appear spontaneous! He seldom meets people socially because he is too shy. "Other 'privately shy' people include politicians, teachers, and entertainers," says Rita. "These people act outgoing when they're doing their jobs, but they're very insecure socially. You'd be amazed how many public figures fit into this category."

Where does shyness come from? Research shows that some people are born with a shy temperament. About 20 percent of babies show abnormal signs of distress when they see strangers or encounter unfamiliar situations. Some scientists feel that such shyness is inherited. "Shy parents are more likely to have shy children than outgoing parents," Rita says. "And shyness can be culturally determined. We know that Japanese and Taiwanese students are statistically shyer than Israeli students."

If 15 to 20 percent of shyness is innate, how do other people become shy? Children may become shy when they enter school or meet new challenges. Adolescents may suffer from an identity crisis and become shy. Adults can become shy when confronted by problems like divorce or job loss. Whatever the reasons, shy people suffer from teasing and well-meaning comments like, "Has the cat got your tongue?" They are often lonely and unhappy in social situations. But researchers say there is hope for shyness. Here are some tips you can use to help yourself.

- Don't be a perfectionist. You don't have to have the funniest joke or the most interesting thing to say before you start a conversation. It's better to set realistic goals.
- Don't think the worst. Don't worry about what will happen. Just open your mouth and say something, and you'll find that things work out better than you expected.
- Learn to take rejection. Everyone gets rejected sometimes in social situations. It's not your fault. It's part of life.
- Learn to relax. Practice some relaxing techniques before you go into a social situation. You'll feel better and have more fun.
- Smile and look at people. If you smile and show you're interested, people will respond and conversation will be easier.

Reading Skills

READING COMPREHENSION

Find <u>four</u> correct ways to complete each sentence.

1. Some characteristics of shy people are

   ✓ blushing and stammering.

   _____ appearing confident.

   _____ feeling ill at ease.

   _____ having butterflies in the stomach.

   _____ appearing spontaneous.

   _____ having a pounding heart.

   _____ acting outgoing.

2. Some things shy people do include

   _____ hiding behind someone.

   _____ acting snobbish.

   _____ acting distressed with strangers.

   _____ meeting new challenges.

   _____ teasing others.

   _____ avoiding others.

   _____ planning social occasions.

3. Some people are shy because

_____ of cultural factors.

_____ they have parents who are outgoing.

_____ they have shy parents.

_____ they have a shy temperament.

_____ they have too many social interactions.

_____ they are facing problems such as job loss.

_____ they are too relaxed.

4. Some ways people can become less shy include

_____ smiling at others.

_____ rejecting others before others reject them.

_____ practicing relaxation techniques.

_____ telling funny jokes.

_____ being perfectionists.

_____ not worrying about what will happen.

_____ learning to accept rejection.

VOCABULARY IN CONTEXT

Find these expressions in the story. Use the context to help you understand the meaning. Circle the letter of the word or phrase with a similar meaning.

1. blushing and stammering

   a. asking for attention   b. showing nervousness

2. fit the stereotype

   a. are a minority   b. are typical

3. have butterflies in the stomach

   a. feel nervous   b. feel sad

4. on the surface

   a. on the top   b. on the outside

5. down to the last detail

   a. very carefully   b. as low as possible

6. spontaneous

   a. planned   b. not planned

7. culturally determined

   a. based on your artistic   b. based on your national
      ability   origin

8. an identity crisis

   a. to be unsure of   b. to be in trouble with
      yourself   the police

9. Has the cat got your tongue?

   a. Why are you so quiet?   b. Are you feeling sick?

10. a perfectionist

    a. a person who tries   b. a person who tries to do
       to be funny   everything perfectly

UNDERSTAND CAUSE AND EFFECT

*Look at the "tips" section of the reading. Match the suggestions
(causes) with the benefits (effects).*

1. Don't be a perfectionist. __c__   a. You'll have more fun.

2. Don't think the worst. _____   b. It's part of life.

3. Learn to take rejection. _____   c. It's better to set realistic
                                           goals.
4. Learn to relax. _____
                                        d. Conversation will be
5. Smile and look at people. _____   easier.

                                        e. You'll find things work
                                           out in the end.

Before You Read

A. Match the items in List A with the examples in List B.

List A

1. a drink __e__
2. an illness ____
3. a prescription ____
4. a type of medicine ____
5. a musical instrument ____
6. a city ____
7. a life event ____
8. a body organ ____
9. a musical group ____
10. a continent ____
11. a composer ____
12. something that makes bread rise ____

List B

a. Edmonton
b. a violin
c. a string quartet
d. a wedding
e. sake
f. Take an aspirin.
g. the liver
h. a pill
i. Asia
j. yeast
k. hypertension
l. Mozart

B. Discuss these questions in groups.

1. How often do you listen to music?
2. What is your favorite kind of music?
3. Are there any special kinds of music that you listen to in the following situations?

   a. You feel tired.   c. You're anxious and stressed.

   b. You feel sad.   d. You feel happy and loving.

4. How does the music make you feel?

A Prescription for Mozart

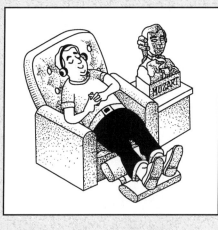

A. Imagine going to your doctor with a complaint of frequent headaches. Your doctor takes a prescription pad and writes a word on it. The word isn't "aspirin," it's "Mozart."

B. The idea isn't so far-fetched. In China, instead of pills, doctors often recommend musical albums with names like *Insomnia* or *Heart, Liver and Lungs*, and Chinese people "take" these musical pieces as prescriptions. In fact, in China music is prescribed as often as herbal medicine to help people with common, everyday problems or to strengthen organs like the liver or the kidneys. Other countries use music for healing as well. In Japan, Mendelssohn's "Spring Song" is often used to treat migraine headaches. And hospitals in India use different kinds of music to treat hypertension and mental illness.

C. Using music as therapy isn't new. It dates back to the beginning of civilization when people got together to play music on primitive drums and rattles. Music plays a part in every ritual and important life event, from weddings and funerals to crop planting and harvesting to marching people into battle. There is even evidence that music was our first language. Scientists found that two-thirds of the tiny hairs inside the human ear respond only to the higher frequencies of music, which shows that people probably sang before they talked.

D. Many kinds of music can stir the imagination and produce strong feeling. For some people, romantic composers such as Chopin and Tchaikovsky enhance feelings of love and compassion. Religious and spiritual music can help some people feel peace or lessen their pain. But one musician seems to have a unique ability to heal the human body—Wolfgang Amadeus Mozart. Scientists have found Mozart's music to be remarkable in its ability to calm its listeners. It can also increase their perceptions, and help them express themselves more clearly.

E. Many amazing cases have been documented using Mozart as a healing aid. For example, a tiny premature baby named Krissy, who weighed just 1½ pounds at birth, was on total life support. Doctors thought she had little chance of survival. Her mother insisted on playing Mozart for Krissy, and thinks it saved her daughter's life. Krissy lived, but she was very small for her age and slower than the average child. At the age of four, she showed an interest in music and her parents gave her violin lessons. To their astonishment, Krissy was able to play musical pieces from memory that were far beyond the ability of an average four-year-old. Playing music helped her improve in all areas of her life.

F. Other stories have emerged about the effect of Mozart's music. Officials in Washington State report that new arrivals from Asia learn English more quickly when they listen to Mozart. In Edmonton, Alberta, Canada, Mozart string quartets in city squares seem to calm pedestrian traffic. Even animals and seemingly inanimate objects respond to Mozart. In France, cows serenaded with Mozart give more milk, and in Japan, the yeast used to make sake is ten times better when it "listens" to Mozart.

G. Why Mozart, rather than Bach or the Beatles? Any kind of music can have an effect on some people. But Mozart has more balance. It isn't too fast or too slow; it's just right. Don Campbell, who wrote a book called *The Mozart Effect™*, says, "It's like food. A hot spicy meal will affect you differently than a sweet dessert. And while you might love these foods, they aren't good for you to eat every day. You need simple, nutritious food on a steady basis. That's the way Mozart is. It's like a nutritionally balanced meal that brings order and harmony to your body."

Reading Skills

READING COMPREHENSION

Complete each sentence with information from the text. The signal words (in bold type) help you understand the kind of information you are trying to find. You will be looking for examples, times, and reasons.

1. In China, musical albums may be recommended as prescriptions **for** _____ common everyday problems _____ .

2. Music is part of rituals and important life events **such as**

   _____

   _____ .

3. What scientists have found about the inner ear makes them think **that** _____

   _____ .

4. The music of Chopin and Tchaikovsky increases feelings **of**

   _____ .

5. Mozart's music is remarkable because of its ability **to**

   _____ .

6. **When** Krissy showed interest in music,

   _____ .

7. **When** new arrivals from Asia listen to Mozart, they

   _____ .

8. Mozart seems to work better than Bach or the Beatles **because**

   _____ .

Use the story context to find the meanings of the underlined words below. Then write the words or ideas they refer to on the lines.

1. Paragraph B: <u>The idea</u> isn't so far fetched

   the word "Mozart" on a prescription pad.

2. Paragraph B: . . . <u>these musical pieces</u> as prescriptions . . .

   _____

3. Paragraph C: <u>It</u> dates back to . . . _____

4. Paragraph D: . . . <u>its</u> ability to calm . . .

   _____

5. Paragraph D: . . . increase <u>their</u> perceptions . . .

   _____

6. Paragraph E: Doctors thought <u>she</u> had . . .

   _____

7. Paragraph E: . . . and thinks <u>it</u> saved . . .

   _____

8. Paragraph F: . . . when <u>they</u> listen to Mozart . . .

   _____

9. Paragraph G: . . . <u>they</u> aren't good for you . . .

   _____

10. Paragraph G: <u>It's</u> like a nutritionally balanced . . .

    _____

VOCABULARY IN CONTEXT

Find these words and expressions in the text and underline them. Use the context to help you understand what they mean. Then underline the word in each row that best expresses the same idea.

1. far-fetched (paragraph B)
   <u>strange</u>   distant   difficult

2. treat (paragraph B)
   help cure   encourage   change

3. therapy (paragraph C)
   entertainment   treatment   stimulation

4. respond (paragraph C)
   notice   hear   react

5. enhance (paragraph D)
   create   provoke   increase

6. heal (paragraph D)
   calm   cure   harm

7. documented (paragraph E)
   recorded   hidden   disproved

8. pedestrian (paragraph F)
   driver   walker   rider

9. inanimate (paragraph F)
   living   not living   moving

10. harmony (paragraph G)
    excitement   health   equilibrium

Put It Together

Match the words that are opposites.

unusual	1. spontaneous _____ planned _____
lower	2. primitive _____
weaken	3. outgoing _____
private	4. heal _____
~~planned~~	5. arrival _____
anxious	6. pedestrian _____
departure	7. public _____
harm	8. common _____
decrease	9. seldom _____
frequently	10. abnormal _____
driver	11. higher _____
self-conscious	12. increase _____
normal	13. strengthen _____
modern	14. relaxed _____

TALK ABOUT IT

Discuss these questions in groups.

1. What are some ways to treat common, everyday health problems?
2. Do the treatments you know about have any risks?
3. Do you know about any alternative treatments? What are they?
4. What do you do when you feel stressed?

5. Do you think it's possible to change your personality if you're shy?

6. How can you make shy people feel at ease?

TELL THE STORIES

A. Tell the story "Has the Cat Got Your Tongue?" Imagine you are a psychologist who works with shy people. Explain:

- what shyness is
- how shy people behave
- how people become shy
- why shyness can be a problem
- some techniques that can help shy people

B. Tell the story "A Prescription for Mozart." Imagine you are a music therapist who uses different kinds of music to help people. Explain how music helps people and how you use Mozart in particular. Discuss how music was used in the past.

WRITING OPTION

Write a composition about your personal relationship with music. Say what kind of music you like to listen to and in what circumstances. What impact does music have on you and what role does it play in your life?

or

Work in a group to write a brochure for shy people, telling them they are not alone and offering suggestions for overcoming their shyness.

BEYOND THE STORIES

Prepare a brief presentation to give to the class about a form of music that is popular in your culture (traditional or modern). Bring a tape to class and play an example of the music.

Making a Difference

STORY 1   DIVING FOR TREASURES

STORY 2   DO YOU SPEAK MY LANGUAGE?

Let's Get Ready

A. Match the words to the meanings.

1. trash ___f___

2. a reservoir _____

3. an interpreter _____

4. frustrated _____

5. dive _____

6. impersonal _____

7. scuba gear _____

8. edge _____

9. stuff _____

10. a rubber raft _____

a. go headfirst into the water

b. detached, not connected

c. equipment for diving underwater

d. something you use to float on the water

e. disappointed and unhappy

f. garbage

g. a translator

h. the place where something ends

i. objects, things

j. a place where water is collected for later use

B. Discuss these questions in groups.

1. What are some problems with our environment today?
2. What are some things people can do to help the environment?
3. How much difference can an individual make?

Before You Read

Use these words to complete the paragraphs.

climbing
Wildman
natural
~~people~~
job
building
eat
strange
man
resources
picked
authorities

In the 843 acres of New York's Central Park there have been some unusual activities and unusual (1) ____people____ —some of them bad, some of them good, and some of them . . . well, just (2) _____. One man spent years (3) _____ into trees and building tree houses in the park. Park authorities spent years finding the structures hidden in the trees and taking them apart without finding the person who was (4) _____ them. Eventually, they came across the (5) _____ sleeping in one of his houses high in the trees. They offered him a (6) _____ helping to maintain the trees in the park.

Another "park person" named himself (7) _____ and began living off the plants that grow in the park. He made soups, salads, and even bread from leaves and berries that he (8) _____. Once Wildman was stopped by park (9) _____ when they saw him pick and eat a dandelion. Wildman wanted to show people that these plants were good to eat. "Don't worry. I promise not to (10) _____ Central Park," Wildman joked. Now he gives guided tours and lectures schoolchildren about the (11) _____ cycles of plants and about conserving the park and its (12) _____.

Diving for Treasures

The Jacqueline Kennedy Onassis Reservoir in New York's Central Park is a favorite place for joggers and romantic couples to meet. But imagine one jogger's surprise when she saw someone in full scuba gear jump out of a yellow rubber raft and disappear into the water! Just as she was about to call for help, another person in scuba gear came up out of the water and dropped a bag into the raft. What was going on?

George and Catherine Parry have been busy with their hobby since 1996. The New York couple have been working to clean up the reservoir in Central Park. Mr. Parry, who met his wife while jogging near the reservoir, says, "We were aware of trash collecting along the edges of the water. Turtles, birds, and ducks were getting caught in the garbage and drowning. We wanted to do something." The first step was trying to contact authorities responsible for the reservoir. The Parrys sent more than 20 letters, but with tight budgets neither the Parks Department nor the Department of Environmental Protection (DEP) responded. Finally, they got an interview with the DEP and a one-month contract to clean the reservoir on their own time with their own equipment.

Cleaning around the edge of the reservoir took the Parrys eight days and countless garbage bags. As they cleaned, they faxed the DEP with reports of their progress. When they mentioned that there seemed to be a lot of stuff underwater, the DEP responded by saying, "Why don't you go down there and take a look around?" George Parry was delighted. He had been scuba diving for years and had taught Catherine to scuba dive in the Caribbean. This was all the encouragement they needed.

From under the water the Parrys brought an amazing collection of things. Thousands of whiskey, soda, and champagne bottles, four basketball hoops, six dead rats, nine Frisbees, more than 100 tennis balls and a dozen rackets, dozens of knives, a dead raccoon, a coffee table, a briefcase, a faceless alarm clock, a toy shovel, and a drowning parakeet they tried unsuccessfully to save. They even found a baby carriage (but no evidence of a baby), a rubber alligator, and ski boots. "We are the only people in New York, or anywhere else, with permission to go swimming in the reservoir," smiles Catherine.

While the Parrys work, passersby often hang over the fence around the reservoir. They watch in fascination and sometimes call out encouragement to the couple cleaning up their park. With a surface area of 110 acres and a depth of 45 feet, who knows what else is down there? The Parrys have found more than garbage in the reservoir. They've seen animal life such as fish, turtles, and small crabs under the water. Still, with all the trash down there, they see a big job ahead. "We may have signed on for a lifelong job," George smiles. "But it's our way of doing something good for our park."

Reading Skills

Skim the story to answer these "WH" questions.

1. WHO: Who are the main characters in this story?

   George and Catherine Parry
   _____

2. WHERE: Where does the story take place?

   _____

3. WHAT: What are they doing that is unusual?

   _____

4. HOW: How are they doing this work?

   _____

5. WHY: Why are they doing this?

   _____

6. WHEN: When did they start and when will they finish?

   _____

Put the events in order.

_____ The Parrys got permission to clean the reservoir on their own time.

_____ The Parrys were upset by the trash that damaged the environment.

_____ The Parrys brought up an amazing collection of things.

_____ The DEP encouraged the Parrys to explore underwater.

__1__ George and Catherine met while jogging around the reservoir.

_____ The Parrys began to write letters to public authorities.

_____ It took eight days to clean the edge of the reservoir.

_____ They may be doing this job for a long time.

RECYCLE THE VOCABULARY

Use the words listed to complete the information below.

fish

~~trash~~

raccoon

scuba diving

parakeet

public

authorities

jogging

dive

crabs

scuba gear

passersby

turtles

rubber raft

rat

citizens

garbage bags

1. another word for <u>garbage</u>: _____ trash _____

2. two sports: _____ _____

3. another word for <u>officials</u>: _____

4. three things the Parrys used for collecting the garbage:

_____ _____

_____

5. three creatures that live in the water: _____

_____ _____

6. a way to say <u>go under the water</u>: _____

7. three land creatures: _____

_____ _____

8. three words for "people": _____

_____ _____

RECALL THE INFORMATION

Work in groups. From memory, make a list of things the Parrys found underwater in the Central Park reservoir. Don't look back at the story for help until you finish your list.

Before You Read

Discuss these questions in groups.

1. Is English an easy language to learn? Explain.
2. When did you first begin to learn English?
3. What is your biggest problem in learning English?
4. What are the biggest problems immigrants have when they don't speak the language?
5. What kind of help can people get in learning a new language?

Do You Speak My Language?

Dr. Jack Chan remembers the first time his father took him to school when he was a young child. "When I saw him leaving, I panicked and started screaming," he recalls. Dr. Chan grew up in a small town in Oregon and learned Chinese at home with his family. He can't forget how terrified he felt when he began kindergarten and realized he couldn't understand English. "Even 20 years later, I remember the feeling that I wouldn't be able to communicate with the teacher and the other students. It was very frightening," he says.

Dr. Chan now works at a health care clinic with patients from different language backgrounds. Many of them don't speak English. To communicate, Dr. Chan often has to resort to body language. "I lift up my shirt, open my mouth, or point to my ears. It can be frustrating for the patients when they can't tell me what's bothering them," he says. "I can understand how they feel. And with over 200 patients using the clinic each day, it can be quite a problem."

Now a new service is changing the way the doctor communicates.

Dr. Chan is using AT&T **Language Line**® Services to talk to his patients over the telephone. "It's great," he says. "At first I was concerned about the impersonal aspect of using a phone, but when I asked my patients how they liked it, they were very positive. They felt relieved to be able to explain their problems and symptoms to me through the interpreter." Dr. Chan continues, "An average well-baby visit takes about 15 minutes, but when English was not the first language, it used to take up to an hour. By the end, we were all angry and frustrated, even the little kids."

More than 1000 people work at Language Line Services, interpreting from English into 140 languages, from Armenian to Vietnamese. The line is available 24 hours a day, 365 days a year. By simply dialing an 800 number, tens of thousands of businesses can access an interpreter within moments to help handle calls from non–English speaking customers. The service provides expert interpreters to help medical care workers, people in business, or anyone who deals with people of different language backgrounds. One interpreter recalls interpreting for an American company doing business in Germany. After an hour on the phone, the company closed a $30-million-dollar deal. The caller said he wanted to come and kiss her, to thank her for her help.

The interpreters are the heart and soul of the service. They must go beyond a word-for-word translation to interpret the true meaning of the message. The interpreters are well educated and have native fluency in English and in the language they interpret. Many have specialties in medical, legal, or business terminology. All the interpreters have stories to tell. "You take a lot of calls in an eight-hour shift. Sometimes you have to deal with strange situations," says one interpreter. He recalls taking a call on a steamy hot day in California, where Language Line Services is based. It was from someone in a freezing cold city in Canada who wanted help calling the power company because his electricity had been disconnected.

But it's not all business. One interpreter recalls how he conducted a romance. "The man was from Texas, and the woman was a 'mail-order bride' in Russia. Things were going well and they were making plans to meet in Moscow. Some of the calls lasted an hour or more, and I could see that the man was falling in love. It was very romantic. Then suddenly the woman changed her mind, and the tone of her voice became chilly. She had decided this man wasn't for her and wanted to call the whole thing off. I had to deliver the brush-off. I felt really awful," he recounts.

It's not easy being part of people's personal lives. Interpreters have heard everything, from business transactions to personal problems. One interpreter had to coach a woman in labor to push harder. The confused woman asked, "Who are you?" But another woman, after an accident that landed her in the hospital, said gratefully, "Language Line Services was a lifesaver."

Reading Skills

*Read the sentences and write **T** for true or **F** for false. Correct the wrong information.*

1. Dr. Chan had a frightening experience when he began kindergarten. __T__

2. Dr. Chan uses body language when his patients don't speak English. _____

3. Many patients didn't like the idea of using the telephone to communicate. _____

4. A baby check-up takes about the same amount of time now as it did before. _____

5. Most of the interpreters help people in the medical profession.

    _____

6. The interpreters try to give a word-for-word translation whenever possible. _____

7. The interpreters have a native fluency in both of the languages they are translating. _____

8. Language Line is based in Canada. _____

9. The interpreter seemed happy that the couple was falling in love. _____

10. The woman in labor was confused about who the interpreter was. _____

USE THE CONTEXT TO FIND THE MEANING

Find the expressions in List A in the story. Then match each expression to an explanation or definition in List B.

List A

1. resort to body language __n__

2. the impersonal aspect of using a phone ____

3. They were very positive. ____

4. a well-baby visit ____

5. the heart and soul of the service ____

6. a word-for-word translation ____

7. native fluency in the language ____

8. an eight-hour shift ____

9. a steamy day ____

10. a mail-order bride ____

11. Her voice became chilly. ____

12. a brush-off ____

13. coach a woman in labor ____

14. landed in the hospital ____

15. a lifesaver ____

List B

a. encourage a woman who is having a baby

b. telling someone you don't want to see him or her anymore

c. a very hot day

d. to translate the exact meaning of each word

e. They liked the idea.

f. something that saves a person's life

g. was sent to the hospital after an accident or illness

h. speak the language very well

i. a check-up for a baby

j. She became uninterested.

k. a workday that lasts eight hours

l. feeling detached from the person you're speaking to

m. the most important part of the service

n. use motions to show something

o. a person you find out about from a catalog

Match the words from the story that go together.

fluency

~~your mind~~

deal

town

translation

shift

language

number

in love

bride

1. change _____your mind_____

2. native _____

3. an eight-hour _____

4. a small _____

5. a mail-order _____

6. body _____

7. an 800 _____

8. a million-dollar _____

9. fall _____

10. a word-for-word _____

Put It Together

Classify the words listed to complete the chart.

	Object	Place	Person	Action
1. rubber raft	✓			
2. interpret				
3. passerby				
4. communicate				
5. kindergarten				
6. reservoir				
7. jogger				
8. collect trash				
9. coffee table				
10. scientist				
11. baby				
12. health care clinic				
13. disconnect				
14. to coach				
15. Moscow				

	Object	Place	Person	Action
16. rowing				
17. wife				
18. equipment				
19. authority				
20. citizen				
21. tennis ball				
22. George Parry				
23. briefcase				
24. New York				
25. deliver				

TALK ABOUT IT

Discuss these questions in groups.

1. How much difference do you think cleaning the reservoir will make?

2. Do you know of any other people who work to make the environment cleaner? Who are they? What do they do?

3. What can individuals do to help the environment?

4. Which things do you personally do?

5. Have you ever been in an emergency situation where you couldn't speak the language? What happened?

6. Would you like to use a telephone interpreter like the ones at Language Line? Explain why or why not.

7. What do you think is the most difficult part of an interpreter's job?

TELL THE STORIES

A. Tell the story "Diving for Treasures." Imagine you are George or Catherine Parry. Explain why you are diving into the reservoir and what you have found. Talk about what the reservoir means to you and how you hope to make a difference.

B. Tell the story "Do You Speak My Language?" Imagine you are one of the interpreters at Language Line and you get all kinds of calls. Describe how Language Line works, who uses it, and how it helps people. Use examples from the text to tell some funny or interesting stories.

WRITING OPTION

Imagine you are George or Catherine Parry and you are writing to the Department of Environmental Protection to complain about the condition of the Central Park reservoir (or some other place you know about). Describe the situation and suggest solutions.

or

Write a composition about what a person feels like when he or she doesn't speak the language well enough to communicate with others.

BEYOND THE STORIES

Identify a problem in your community or in the neighborhood around the school where you study English. Work in a group to plan a campaign to find a solution to the problem. Identify people you can contact, including officials responsible for that problem. In your group, plan a course of action that could make a difference.

ANSWER KEY

Unit 1   Against the Odds

STORY 1   HOW A POWER DRILL SAVED A LIFE

Before You Read   *Page 2*

2. remote   5. rooms   8. plane
3. people   6. surgery   9. land
4. clinic   7. city   10. emergency

Reading Skills

FOCUS ON THE EXACT INFORMATION   *Page 5*

2. by a rock   8. brain surgery
3. operation / save his life   9. around the patient
4. was urgent   10. They made a hole
5. immediate surgery   11. around the huge hole
6. fogged in   12. waking up
7. would stop breathing

VOCABULARY IN CONTEXT   *Page 6*

2. fogged in   5. critical   8. decision   11. skull
3. arrive   6. transferred   9. breathing   12. a life
4. emergency   7. pressure   10. ordinary

BUILD YOUR VOCABULARY   *Page 7*

2. S   5. S   8. S
3. S   6. A   9. S
4. A   7. A   10. S

STORY 2   HE'S ALIVE!

Before You Read   *Page 8*

A.

2. T   3. F   4. T   5. F   6. F

Reading Skills

READING COMPREHENSION *Page 11*

5, 3, 1, 8, 2, 6, 10, 4, 7, 9

REVIEW THE VOCABULARY *Page 12*

2. hike	5. shelter	8. exhausted
3. blow	6. alive	9. relief
4. place	7. cheers	10. wrapper

RECYCLE THE VOCABULARY *Page 12*

2. waists	5. chin	7. ankle
3. foot	6. wrist	8. hand
4. arm		

Put It Together

LET'S REVIEW *Page 13*

2. lot	5. climber	8. shop
3. bar	6. worker	9. drill
4. wind	7. ankle	10. situation

Unit 2   The Wave of the Future

Let's Get Ready   *Page 15*

A.

expensive, strong, competition, boring

B.

2. A   3. S   4. S   5. A   6. S

> STORY 1   X-SPORTS

Reading Skills

FOCUS ON THE EXACT INFORMATION   *Page 19*

2. rage, juice, energy	7. thrill
3. to the edge as possible	8. the appeal
4. extreme sports	9. boring
5. risk / excitement	10. potential / huge
6. more expensive sports	

REVIEW THE VOCABULARY *Page 20*

2. in 4. over 6. up 8. of
3. to 5. down 7. from

BUILD YOUR VOCABULARY *Page 21*

2. edge 5. boring 8. challenge
3. risk 6. equipment 9. rent
4. alternative 7. skill 10. ride

STORY 2   PAGE ME!

Reading Skills

SCAN FOR THE DETAILS *Page 25*

2. Doctors and other professionals
3. Working parents
4. Teenagers
5. The codes
6. Julia Rodriguez
7. Julia's friends and her boyfriend
8. Manufacturers
9. Service charges
10. Older customers

REVIEW THE EXPRESSIONS *Page 26*

2. pager
3. become popular
4. contact
5. very trendy
6. the newest
7. translate into language
8. cheap
9. be part of
10. telephone

USE THE CONTEXT TO FIND THE MEANING *Page 26*

2. pagers
3. teenagers
4. some teens
5. Julia's friends and her boyfriend
6. pagers
7. pagers
8. fluorescent, glow-in-the-dark, and transparent pagers
9. a company / another company
10. the pager

Put It Together

LET'S REVIEW   *Page 27*

2. c	5. d	7. b
3. a	6. g	8. f
4. h		

Unit 3   Looking Good

Let's Get Ready   *Page 30*

2. k	6. j	10. g
3. l	7. h	11. c
4. d	8. a	12. i
5. b	9. f	

STORY 1   THE MOST BEAUTIFUL WOMEN IN THE WORLD

Before You Read   *Page 32*

B.

Positive: pride, honored, admire, winner, fortunately, advantage, opportunity
Negative: silly, sacrifice, starve, obsession

Reading Skills

READ FOR THE MAIN IDEAS   *Page 34*

2. E	4. D	6. F
3. C	5. A	

READING COMPREHENSION   *Page 35*

2. b	4. a	6. a
3. a	5. c	

BUILD YOUR VOCABULARY   *Page 36*

2. c	5. f	8. b	11. h
3. a	6. k	9. d	12. l
4. g	7. e	10. j	

UNDERSTAND FACT AND OPINION *Page 37*

2. F	5. F	8. F
3. O	6. O	9. O
4. O	7. F	10. O

RECYCLE THE VOCABULARY *Page 38*

Across
- 2. sacrifice
- 4. beautiful
- 5. stretch
- 6. pride
- 8. absence
- 10. starve
- 12. opportunity
- 13. diet
- 14. plastic

Down
- 1. frequently
- 2. silly
- 3. immediately
- 7. effort
- 9. straighten
- 11. title
- 12. obsession

STORY 2   GETTING PIERCED

Reading Skills

READING COMPREHENSION *Page 42*

2. T	5. T	8. F	11. T
3. F	6. F	9. T	12. T
4. F	7. F	10. F	

SCAN FOR THE DETAILS *Page 43*

- 2. Pierre Black
- 3. Sacha
- 4. Couples
- 5. Rich women
- 6. People in India
- 7. Group members
- 8. Pierre Black
- 9. A young woman
- 10. Some people

REVIEW THE VOCABULARY *Page 44*

tongue	6	lip	5	web between thumb	9
nose	4	cheek	3	and forefinger	
ear	2	elbow	7		
navel	8				

SKIM TO CHECK THE INFORMATION *Page 44*

1, 3, 4, 7, 8, 9, 10, 12, 14, 15

Put It Together

    2. Preparing for beauty contests is a full-time job for six months.
3. Many people associate body piercing with street kids.
4. Pierre insists that body piercing is safe if done properly.
5. Couples get pierced to show their commitment to each other.
6. The beauty contestants sacrifice time and money for the contests.

Unit 4   Outer Space

Let's Get Ready   *Page 48*

A.

2. e	5. b	8. f	11. g
3. j	6. h	9. a	12. k
4. l	7. d	10. c	

STORY 1   CRUMBS FROM HEAVEN

Before You Read   *Page 50*

Large: spaceship, rock, planet, meteor, heaven, desert
Small: speck, dust, rock, trinket, slice, pebble, crumb, particle

Reading Skills

READING COMPREHENSION   *Page 52*

    2. from $2,000 to $40,000
3. People want any kind of material from the sky.
4. when the Pathfinder spaceship returned with reports of primitive life on Mars
5. watching pictures from Mars
6. from $60 to over $2,000
7. They think they will outperform the stock market.
8. They can't afford them.
9. You have to study the whole object.
10. He put the particles in plastic cubes.

SCAN FOR THE DETAILS   *Page 53*

    2. A 16-inch meteorite
3. a spaceship that landed on Mars

4. $1,000 per gram
5. 4,000 viewers of a home shopping channel
6. rocks and gems
7. $30,000
8. Research scientists
9. earrings and trinkets
10. rocks from a driveway, crumbs

VOCABULARY IN CONTEXT   *Page 54*

2. a	4. b	6. b	8. b	10. b
3. a	5. b	7. a	9. b	

STORY 2   WHO'S OUT THERE?

Reading Skills

SKIM TO CHECK THE INFORMATION   *Page 59*

2. T
3. F (Most people have the same idea.)
4. F (a flying disk or saucer)
5. T
6. T
7. F (They were just happy to be there.)
8. F (one-quarter)
9. T
10. F (Some just don't know.)

UNDERSTAND THE MAIN IDEAS AND DETAILS   *Page 60*

a survey about life in outer space
rumors that began in 1947
new rumors in the 1980s
gathering in Roswell, New Mexico
people making money from alien stories

READING COMPREHENSION   *Page 62*

6, 9, 3, 8, 5, 1, 2, 7, 4, 10

SCAN FOR THE DETAILS   *Page 63*

2. 1947	5. 110°	8. 40%
3. 1980s	6. 4th	9. 50%
4. 100,000	7. 900	10. 85%

Put It Together

LET'S REVIEW   *Page 64*

1. tall, slender, friendly, visit regularly, huge heads, intelligent, almond-shaped eyes, come in spaceships
2. look like rocks, found in African desert, come from Mars, sold in plastic cubes, black, sell at auctions, are made into trinkets, are complex things, have gone up in price
3. alien refrigerator magnets, alien-based movies, stuffed alien dolls, meteorites for investment, viewing a spaceship landing site, specks of meteorites, meteorite jewelry and trinkets, meteorite particles in cubes

Unit 5   A New Beginning

Let's Get Ready   *Page 68*

2. c	4. c	6. c	8. a
3. b	5. a	7. b	

STORY 1   A LUCKY TIME TO GET MARRIED

Before You Read   *Page 70*

B.

2. stamp, envelope
3. aunt, sister
4. couple, bride

5. customs, rituals
6. Roman, Chinese

Reading Skills

READING COMPREHENSION   *Page 72*

2. It's the most popular day to get married in China.
3. People begin new lives together. Families are joined.
4. an anthropologist who studies weddings
5. something old, something blue
6. something borrowed
7. to confuse evil spirits
8. They had strong-smelling herbs to scare away witches and devils.
9. May 18
10. hairdressers, florists, and owners of restaurants and limousine services

SKIM TO CHECK THE INFORMATION   *Page 74*

2. F (in May)
3. T
4. T
5. T

6. T
7. F (old)
8. F (the Romans carried . . .)
9. F (new tradition)

10. F "I will be rich."
11. F (not everyone)
12. T

BUILD YOUR VOCABULARY   *Page 75*

2. h
3. d

4. f
5. j

6. i
7. e

8. c
9. a

10. b

RECYCLE THE VOCABULARY   *Page 75*

2. banquet
3. reception
4. prices

5. spirits
6. bridesmaid
7. feelings

8. confuse
9. bouquet
10. day

STORY 2   CREATING HARMONY

Reading Skills

READ FOR THE MAIN IDEA   *Page 78*

c

READING COMPREHENSION   *Page 78*

1. an American Indian ritual.
   similar to a Greek ritual.
   a way to get rid of negativity.
2. lighting a strong-smelling herb.
   putting out oils and crystals.
   chanting a song.
   using a laundry liquid called bluing.
3. an ancient folk art.
   concerned with the correct placement of objects.
   designed to bring harmony and good luck.
   becoming well known in western cultures.
4. painting rooms certain colors.
   putting mirrors near doors.
   putting plants in entrance ways.
   the correct placement of objects.
5. feeling more in harmony with others.
   getting along better with others.
   feeling cozy and satisfied.
   feeling different.

ANSWER KEY

2. b	5. b	8. b
3. a	6. b	9. b
4. a	7. a	10. a

RECYCLE THE VOCABULARY *Page 81*

2. a	5. c	8. f	11. k
3. j	6. d	9. l	12. g
4. b	7. e	10. h	

Put It Together

LET'S REVIEW *Page 82*

A.

2. c   3. a   4. g   5. h   6. e   7. b   8. f

B.

Belief or Tradition: 6, 13   Object: 5, 7, 9, 10, 17, 19
Action: 8, 12, 15, 16   Place: 3, 11, 18
Feeling: 4, 14, 20

Unit 6 Heroes

STORY 1 NEVER STOP MOVING

Reading Skills

FOCUS ON THE EXACT INFORMATION *Page 89*

2. professional job
3. lost control
4. never walk again
5. stop moving
6. stand / support
7. brother-in-law
8. whole body
9. audition
10. partially paralyzed
11. fall down during the filming
12. dancers / actors / athletes

VOCABULARY IN CONTEXT *Page 90*

1. terrible
2. amateur, always
3. rainy, unconscious
4. dead, loved
5. left, crying
6. persisted, beautiful
7. major, partially
8. flexible, famous
9. friends, first

UNDERSTAND FACT AND OPINION   *Page 91*

2. F	5. O	8. F
3. O	6. F	9. O
4. O	7. O	10. O

STORY 2   SEARCH-AND-RESCUE MOM

Reading Skills

SKIM FOR THE MAIN IDEAS   *Page 94*

2. B	4. C	6. G
3. D	5. A	7. F

READING COMPREHENSION   *Page 95*

1. puts on her red jacket.
   calls her dog, Aly.
   says good-bye to her children.
2. Caroline became exhausted.
   it was dark.
   Aly couldn't find the scent in the cold.
3. she is a natural athlete.
   she likes to help people.
   she likes physical challenges.
4. they make a great team.
   Caroline can translate for other rescue workers.
   Caroline and Aly can find people faster than other searchers.

RECYCLE THE VOCABULARY   *Page 96*

2. human	4. lost	6. situation
3. nurse	5. hobby	

Put It Together

LET'S REVIEW   *Page 97*

2. f	5. a	8. c
3. e	6. d	9. b
4. h	7. g	10. i

Unit 7 Technoworld

STORY 1 THE WORLD IS GETTING SMALLER

Before You Read *Page 102*

2. minute   microscopic
3. globe   world
4. operation   injection
5. industry   factories
6. heart   arteries

Reading Skills

SKIM FOR THE MAIN IDEAS *Page 104*

A.

1. C
2. D
3. B
4. F
5. H
6. E
7. G

B.

C: How small are . . .
D: nanobots will revolutionize manufacturing
B: Nanotechnology is the science . . .
F: medical science
H: When could all of this happen?
E: environment
G: tiny machines in surgery

UNDERSTAND CAUSE AND EFFECT *Page 105*

2. e	4. c	6. f	8. a
3. h	5. b	7. d	

VOCABULARY IN CONTEXT *Page 106*

2. b	5. b	8. a	11. b
3. b	6. a	9. a	12. b
4. a	7. a	10. a	

STORY 2 THE MACHINE THAT KNOWS YOUR FACE

Before You Read *Page 108*

B.

2. c   3. d   4. e   5. a   6. b

Reading Skills

READING COMPREHENSION *Page 111*

2. because the costs are lower than before
3. They worry that the machines will get personal information about them.
4. They can identify criminals or terrorists at airports.
5. They associate fingerprints with criminals.
6. The subject doesn't have to do anything.
7. Students often lost or forgot their cards.
8. Students never forget their hands.
9. Voice recognition is not precise, and can be tricked.
10. if people dye their hair or gain weight
11. New technology can scan the iris of the eye to identify people.
12. a bank card or PIN

USE THE CONTEXT TO FIND THE MEANING *Page 112*

2. biometric
3. some people
4. biometric machines
5. some people
6. fingerprints
7. voice recognition
8. machines fooled by hair dye or weight gain
9. a newer machine
10. your check

ARGUMENTS FOR AND AGAINST *Page 113*

For Biometrics: 2, 3, 6, 9, 10   Against Biometrics: 4, 5, 7, 8

Put It Together

LET'S REVIEW *Page 114*

Across	Down
4. globe	1. recognition
5. swallow	2. revolutionize
7. transport	3. fingerprint
9. teller	5. scientists
11. password	6. arteries
12. biometrics	8. cafeteria
	10. virus

Unit 8   Paradise Lost

STORY 1   CAN YOU COPYRIGHT PARADISE?

Reading Skills

SKIM FOR THE MAIN IDEAS   *Page 122*

2. B	4. F	6. E
3. G	5. D	

READING COMPREHENSION   *Page 123*

2. b	5. c	7. a
3. b	6. c	8. c
4. a		

VOCABULARY IN CONTEXT   *Page 124*

1. countless	5. virtually
2. novels	a proposal
desirable	6. overseas
3. tourists	the aim
rave	7. ruin
4. countryside	for humanity
support	

RECYCLE THE VOCABULARY   *Page 125*

2. villages	7. heritage
3. paintings	8. agency
4. cars	9. oil
5. lines	10. paper
6. names	

STORY 2   THE LAST FRONTIER

Before You Read   *Page 126*

C.

2. F	5. T	8. T
3. T	6. F	9. F
4. T	7. T	10. T

Reading Skills

ARGUMENTS FOR AND AGAINST *Page 129*

Evidence of a remote frontier: 3, 5, 7, 8, 10, 11, 13
Evidence of typical America: 2, 4, 6, 9, 12, 14

CLASSIFY THE EXAMPLES *Page 130*

2. h	5. d	8. b
3. e	6. j	9. c
4. f	7. a	10. g

VOCABULARY IN CONTEXT *Page 130*

2. metropolitan	4. huge	6. expanding
3. remote	resident	attracts
evening	5. divided	7. easier

Put It Together

LET'S REVIEW *Page 131*

2. Half of Alaska's residents now live in metropolitan areas.
3. Tuscany has remained virtually untouched since the Middle Ages.
4. There is still a lot of space in Alaska.
5. Tuscan Square features many products from the region.
6. Moose and elk often wander into people's back yards.

Unit 9   How Do You Feel?

Let's Get Ready   *Page 134*

2. e	4. g	6. a
3. b	5. d	7. c

STORY 1   HAS THE CAT GOT YOUR TONGUE?

Before You Read   *Page 136*

C.

2. F	5. T	8. T
3. T	6. F	9. T
4. F	7. T	10. F

Reading Skills

READING COMPREHENSION   *Page 139*

1. feeling ill at ease.
   having butterflies in the stomach.
   having a pounding heart.
2. hiding behind someone.
   acting snobbish.
   acting distressed with strangers.
   avoiding others.
3. of cultural factors.
   they have shy parents.
   they have a shy temperament.
   they are facing problems such as job loss.
4. smiling at others.
   practicing relaxation techniques.
   not worrying about what will happen.
   learning to accept rejection.

VOCABULARY IN CONTEXT   *Page 140*

2. b	5. a	8. a
3. a	6. b	9. a
4. b	7. b	10. b

UNDERSTAND CAUSE AND EFFECT   *Page 141*

2. e	3. b	4. a	5. d

| STORY 2   A PRESCRIPTION FOR MOZART |

Before You Read   *Page 142*

A.

2. k	5. b	8. g	11. l
3. f	6. a	9. c	12. j
4. h	7. d	10. i	

Reading Skills

READING COMPREHENSION   *Page 145*

2. weddings, funerals, crop planting, harvesting, battles
3. people probably sang before they talked
4. love and compassion

184   **AMAZING STORIES TO TELL AND RETELL 3**

5. calm its listeners
6. her parents gave her violin lessons
7. learn English more quickly
8. It has more balance

USE THE CONTEXT TO FIND THE MEANING   *Page 146*

2. musical albums with names like *Insomnia*
3. using music as therapy
4. Mozart's music
5. listeners'
6. Krissy
7. Mozart's music
8. new arrivals from Asia
9. a hot spicy meal, a sweet dessert
10. Mozart's music

VOCABULARY IN CONTEXT   *Page 147*

2. help cure	5. increase	8. walker
3. treatment	6. cure	9. not living
4. react	7. recorded	10. equilibrium

Put It Together

LET'S REVIEW   *Page 148*

2. modern
3. self-conscious
4. harm
5. departure
6. driver
7. private
8. unusual
9. frequently
10. normal
11. lower
12. decrease
13. weaken
14. anxious

Unit 10   Making a Difference

Let's Get Ready   *Page 150*

A.

2. j	5. a	8. h
3. g	6. b	9. i
4. e	7. c	10. d

Before You Read   *Page 152*

2. strange
3. climbing
4. building
5. man
6. job
7. Wildman

8. picked
9. authorities
10. eat
11. natural
12. resources

Reading Skills

SKIM FOR THE MAIN IDEAS   *Page 155*

2. in Central Park in New York City
3. diving to clean the Central Park reservoir
4. by scuba diving from a rubber raft
5. It's their way of doing something good for their park.
6. 1996 / "It may be a lifelong job."

READING COMPREHENSION   *Page 156*

4, 2, 7, 6, 1, 3, 5, 8

RECYCLE THE VOCABULARY   *Page 157*

2. scuba diving, jogging
3. authorities
4. scuba gear, rubber raft, garbage bags
5. fish, crabs, turtles
6. dive
7. raccoon, parakeet, rat
8. public, passersby, citizens

RECALL THE INFORMATION   *Page 157*

whiskey, soda, and champagne bottles, basketball hoops, dead rats, Frisbees, tennis balls and rackets, knives, a dead raccoon, a coffee table, a briefcase, a faceless alarm clock, a toy shovel, a drowning parakeet, a baby carriage, a rubber alligator, ski boots

Reading Skills

READING COMPREHENSION   *Page 161*

2. T
3. F (They liked the idea.)
4. F (It took longer before.)
5. F (They help people in all professions and businesses.)
6. F (They try to interpret the true meaning of the message.)
7. T
8. F (It is based in California.)
9. T
10. T

USE THE CONTEXT TO FIND THE MEANING   *Page 162*

2. l	6. d	10. o	13. a
3. e	7. h	11. j	14. g
4. i	8. k	12. b	15. f
5. m	9. c		

RECYCLE THE VOCABULARY   *Page 163*

2. fluency	5. bride	8. deal
3. shift	6. language	9. in love
4. town	7. number	10. translation

Put It Together

LET'S REVIEW   *Page 164*

Object: 9, 18, 21, 23
Place: 5, 6, 12, 15, 24
Person: 3, 7, 10, 11, 17, 19, 20, 22
Action: 2, 4, 8, 13, 14, 16, 25